Overcome Parental Burnout

Overcome Parental Burnout © 2025 Deborah Byrne

All rights reserved. No part of this book may be reproduced in any form or by any electronic or mechanical means including information storage and retrieval systems, without permission in writing from the author. The only exception is by a reviewer, who may quote short excerpts in a review.

This is a work of non-fiction. The events and conversations in this book have been set down to the best of the author's ability, although some names and details may have been changed to protect the privacy of individuals. Every effort has been made to trace or contact all copyright holders. The author will be pleased to make good any omissions or rectify any mistakes brought to their attention at the earliest opportunity.

Cover and internal design by Coven Press

Second edition May 2025

www.deborahbyrne.com

Paperback ISBN 978-1-7638641-0-8

eBook ISBN 978-1-7638641-1-5

The author acknowledges the traditional owners of the land and pays respects to Elders, past, present and future.

A catalogue record for this work is available from the National Library of Australia

Overcome Parental Burnout

DEBORAH BYRNE

Overcome Burnout

DEBORAH BYRNE

*This book is dedicated to my darling daughter, Grace.
May you always feel free to be who you are
and know I will always love you.*

INTRODUCTION

The last thing any pregnant woman wants to hear is that her baby has very little chance of survival. However, when I first met with my fertility specialist, while she said the fact I was pregnant was nothing short of a miracle, it was unlikely I would ever be able to hold my baby.

I had recently been diagnosed with Cushing's disease, a rare endocrine disorder that meant my body produced an excess of cortisol. Symptoms included fertility problems, so my appointment with the fertility doctor was originally intended to discuss the possibility of freezing my eggs. Instead, my daughter Grace was on her way.

Much as it was hard to hear an expert tell me it was unlikely my baby would live, I had to face that possibility given the wide range of symptoms I was experiencing. Most seriously, Cushing's had caused me to develop a brain tumour. I was scheduled to have elective brain surgery, which would have a further negative impact on my ability to conceive.

It was yet another blow after two years of fighting with the medical profession to find the reason for all my symptoms. I'd lost almost half my hair, but because I had naturally thick hair, doctors couldn't physically see any difference. Sleep eluded me and I'd stopped menstruating. I had put on a lot of weight with no explanation, but since I'd been a slim size 6 before, nobody could see a problem with the fact that I was now a size 10, even though my diet hadn't changed.

All my concerns were dismissed as being the result of stress from my job as a parenting coach working with foster children. I was given antidepressants and told to rest. It is true my job was stressful. I got up at 5am every morning to support traumatised children who were in the foster care system. It wasn't unusual for me to come home covered in bites and bruises. At the time, I was working closely with a 2-year-old boy who had been through terrible abuse and his 4-year-old foster brother. That 2-year-old had been through a lot in his little life and his behaviour was highly challenging as a result.

Yes, it was hard work, but nothing I hadn't seen before. I'd been doing this kind of work for years. I didn't see why it would suddenly be causing all these problems now when I'd coped fine before. But all the doctors could tell me was slow down, do less, don't worry, forget about it.

I knew in my gut they were wrong.

Eventually, I went to my GP with a proposal. I'd done months of research and knew that a simple blood test would confirm my suspicions. He'd wanted to put me on medication for suspected polycystic ovaries, so I said if they did the tests and they came back negative, I'd accept the diagnosis and take the pills.

He agreed and when the results came back, I learned I had a brain tumour. That news was hard to hear, but at the same time, it was a real relief to have confirmation that I wasn't depressed or overworked. There was an explanation for everything I'd experienced.

I was referred to a specialist, which is what led to me sitting in the office of a fertility expert, discovering that against all the odds, I was pregnant.

Having a high-risk pregnancy, what should have been a magical time of joy and expectation was non-stop stress and worry. I had to have appointments with consultants almost every two weeks to track my baby's progress and make sure she was still alive.

I wanted to look forward to meeting my baby when she was born, but I couldn't make any plans in case I lost her. I couldn't let myself get too close. The thought of losing her made my heart ache; I couldn't add to that pain by bonding with my child.

There was another complication. As soon as I gave birth, I was going to immediately have the brain surgery that had been delayed by my pregnancy. My child might survive only to lose her mother.

It didn't bear thinking about.

I'd wanted nothing more than to be a mum. I'd been a parenting coach for years and looked forward to holding my child in my arms. I had a vision of how blissful those first few weeks would be as we got to know each other, days filled with hugs and kisses. It was a real shock to the system when I developed parental burnout instead.

As I started planning this book, I was living in Melbourne, Australia, a city that had incredibly strict Covid restrictions. This was not the world I wanted to bring a child into.

My child should have been welcomed into the world by her loving family, getting to know the relatives who would love her, just as much as I did. Instead, we were on our own, since her father was no longer involved.

Holding my newborn, I wanted nothing more than to cry my heart out. I felt I'd let her down when her life had barely begun. I couldn't see how I could look after her as well as deal with all my health issues.

I felt like a huge failure. I beat myself up all the more because I felt like I should have taken to mothering with natural ease. I was a parenting coach! I'd seen it all! Why couldn't I be the mother my child needed me to be?

With the benefit of hindsight, I know now that my health

problems were contributing a lot to why I was feeling so bad, but there was more to it than my physical issues. I was on a negative, depressing cycle and there were times when I felt maybe Grace would be better off without me. Having those thoughts compounded those feelings of failure because I felt no good mother would ever think that way and so the downward spiral continued.

As a professional holistic therapist, I know suicidal thoughts are a symptom of emotional flooding, but all the theory didn't make any difference to my lived experience.

8th November 2020 is a date I'll never forget. I finally had my brain surgery.

It had been a long time coming. With all the delays caused by misdiagnoses, I'd been put to the top of the waiting list, but then Covid hit, pushing things back even further. It had taken a year for me to go into surgery, one of the worst years of my life. Perhaps one day I'll write about all those experiences but suffice to say my personal life had completely fallen apart and I felt like I had no strong foundation or support. It was a dark time indeed, but now I'm grateful because it shaped me into the woman I am today.

The prospect of surgery terrified me, not because I was worried anything would go wrong, but because I would have to be separated from my daughter for the five days following it. Any new mum will tell you the last thing they want is to be away from their baby and while I tried to focus on the positives and remind myself it was safest for her to be away from the hospital and any risk of Covid, I still hated the idea of not being able to see her for so long.

The surgery went well, so when I came out of the anaesthetic, all that was left for me to do was lie in a hospital bed, staring at the ceiling as my body recovered. With nothing to do but think, I spent five days examining my life from all directions, questioning why I'd been through all the trials I had, looking for the lessons in every challenge. It didn't take me long to realise I could either continue to feel sorry for myself and fall even further down the well of despair, or I could take this opportunity to start a new chapter with a new attitude.

My parents both worked in the public health sector and if I learned one thing from them, it was that the most precious thing any of us has is time. How you choose to invest that important resource makes all the difference. I'd spent hours sitting with the elderly people my mother cared for and the one common theme to all their stories was they wished they'd spent more time with their family.

My way ahead was clear. Being away from my child for almost a week was a strong reminder of just how much I adored my daughter and how lucky I was to have her when no one thought I'd ever get pregnant, let alone give birth to a healthy baby.

Those five days gave me the chance to discover my life purpose and fulfill the role I was put on this earth to do. Before Grace was born, I had the luxury of going home and recharging after a long day of dealing with other family's challenges. Now I was on call 24/7 and that lack of downtime is a major cause of parental burnout for so many parents. I'd been hit by parental burnout within days of my daughter arriving and I needed to figure out how to overcome it.

Going into surgery, I'd been convinced I'd let both myself and Grace down, but when I left the hospital, I was filled with a new feeling of fearlessness. I knew what I had to do:

- Be the best possible mother to Grace. I might not be perfect, but no mother is. I could still be the best mother for her.
- I was told it would take me a year to recover from my surgery, so I was going to use that time to heal myself on every level. From now on, I would live in the present

moment, move past any feelings of guilt and enjoy every aspect of motherhood, warts and all.
- Support as many parents as I could, no matter where they were on the planet, so they could enjoy strong relationships with their children, cope effectively with stress and avoid suffering from parental burnout.

This realisation is what led me to create the Focused Family Formula. I used to work as a holistic therapist and I had many qualifications in a range of techniques, including hypnotherapy and neuro-linguistic programming (NLP). I drew upon everything I'd learned and combined it with my years of experience as a parenting coach to start working on myself and bring those techniques to others.

I knew the first thing I had to sort out was my time management. Most parents will tell you; they feel like they're constantly rushing from one appointment to another, always under pressure to get everything done, yet never feeling like they've made any progress.

I began to declutter my life. On a superficial level this involved cutting out anything I didn't need to do from my schedule, but I took this process much further. I let go of anything that was out of my control. I had no power over what other people said or did, so I stopped trying to change them to suit me. Instead, I started to embody acceptance, mindfulness and self-forgiveness, treating myself with the same kind of loving kindness I gave my daughter. My journey into motherhood had had a rocky start, but I couldn't change the past. But I could make sure that the future looked very different.

My self-care routine became an essential rather than a luxury. As a single parent to a baby, this could be hard since her needs always came first. But I looked for ways to take care of myself even on difficult days. If there were times when all I could do was curl up in bed and give Grace a cuddle, I gave myself full permission to do this and enjoyed every moment. The chores could wait until tomorrow. After all, if I had a friend who was recovering from brain surgery, I'd be telling her to take it easy, so I was finally taking my own advice.

Did you know just five minutes of meditation has a positive impact on the brain?[1] On days when I only had five minutes to grab a quick break, I spent that time practicing mindfulness or focusing on my breath to give my brain a little break and recharge it.

I forgave myself for not being the ideal mother I had dreamed of being. There has never been more pressure on parents to be perfect all the time with beautifully turned-out children and a wonderfully clean and tidy house. Newsflash – it's an impossible goal! The second I stopped putting pressure on myself to live up to an unrealistic expectation, I immediately felt much more relaxed.

As a parenting coach, I'd already known all about this stuff, but I'd let it slide because I'd been feeling so burnt out. Now I fully embraced all the tools I'd been giving to families for years. I made more time for myself so I could spend more quality time with Grace. I promised myself I was going to spend my year of recovery to fully step into the woman and mother I was born to be. Being sick forced me to take a break and take stock of my life. I honestly believe if I hadn't taken the time to learn all those essential lessons, my health would have gone further downhill.

Another major change was deciding to change the direction of my career. It was time for me to transition into full-time parenting coach with my Focused Family Formula. This also meant I could help families around the world, thanks to the wonders of the internet.

I've always loved working with troubled families. I get such a buzz from seeing a child turn a corner. Being a small part of their lives, supporting them to grow and giving their parents powerful tools to do the same is the most rewarding work there is. I've worked with many, many people over the years, dealing with organisations, schools and families, but I've always felt driven to do even more.

My time out enabled me to see there was a lot of repetition to most of my work. I realised I could take that work and pour it into an online parenting course that would have a universal appeal. I might not have had much money and I might not be particularly technologically minded, but I was fuelled by passion, and I got straight into it.

I ended up creating a 12-week online program inspired by all the principles I'd been using as a parenting coach and that I've been following with my own daughter. I knew that course was going to change so many lives for the better, but it wasn't enough for me. I wanted to reach even more people, help those who might not be ready for the course but still needed some guidance.

That's why I've written this book. In the following pages you will learn all about many of the principles that are covered in greater depth in the Focused Family Formula. You'll discover a number of techniques and strategies to help you develop healthier relationships with your children.

Each chapter contains several funny stories from my time as a parenting coach and my personal experiences as a mother to show you the problems you have are universal. You are not alone! Then I'll go into evidence-based methods you can use to solve those problems, giving you practical advice you can start applying right away. I've personally seen the positive impact of what I'm going to share with you and I'm so excited to be able to help you enjoy the same transformation.

The first year of my daughter's life was a difficult one, filled with hard work and self-development. But everything I learned from that year has made such a difference.

Now I'm the proud mother of a beautiful, adorable daughter, nothing like the burnt-out wreck I was in the early days. We are incredibly close and our relationship goes from strength to strength. I live in the present moment, not worrying about the future or beating myself up about the past. I manage my time effectively, so I have plenty of hours for the most important things in life. I've found the secret to a work/life balance, and I help parents all around the world with my Focused Family Formula.

Since it's so important to me to give back to the community, I work with a number of charity organisations and offer scholarships to families facing homelessness so they can use the Focused Family Formula to support them through those difficult times. In addition, all the profits from this book will go to charity.

I'm so grateful for my health problems now. They were what allowed me to find my purpose. I still have issues with my health, but they don't overwhelm me. Likewise, I know it would be easy to slide back into depression, but now I have an effective plan to deal with negative thoughts if they occur.

I want you to know you can find the same level of inner peace. It all starts with a focused mindset, which is what we're going to examine in the first chapter.

If you're ready to make a change for the better, turn the page and read on. A new life awaits!

CHAPTER ONE

what on earth has happened to me?

My self-care routine today consisted of letting the steam hit my face after the dishwasher cycle – Unknown

As a single parent to a small child, I can't always go out to celebrate special occasions. While I work hard to appreciate every moment, I'll stick my hand up to feeling sorry for myself at times – especially when it's my birthday and Covid means I couldn't go anywhere exciting.

Since we had such strict Covid rules in Australia, getting together with friends and family was completely out of the question. Grace wasn't really old enough to understand birthdays, so I'd had to content myself with cards in the post and a Zoom chat with my mother.

Alone with only a boisterous toddler for company, I decided to treat myself to the ultimate comfort food – a huge pizza with stuffed crust and all the sides! I put in the call and played with Grace while I waited for my food to arrive. My daughter was at her absolute cutest, but I was struggling to raise a smile as we played hide and seek. Grace would crouch down behind a chair, giggling and giving away her location even before she called out to me, 'I'm over here, Mummy!'

I'd dutifully pretend I couldn't see her, giving an exaggerated cry of delight when I finally went round the chair to discover her. It was fun, but hardly the birthday party I'd hoped for.

I'd so needed something special after everything I'd been through, so when the doorbell rang to let me know my pizza was there, I was glad for the excuse to stop playing.

'I'm hiding, Mummy!' Grace told me as I went to the door to collect the pizza.

I'll confess that my attention wasn't fully on our game. My mind was thinking about the delicious pizza I was about to eat. It might not have been the greatest birthday ever, but at least *something* good was going to come out of it.

I sat down at the dining table and selected a large slice of pizza. I'd lost my sense of smell and taste post surgery, but that wasn't going to stop me savouring this rare treat.

I closed my eyes for a moment and imagined the scent of melted cheese and pepperoni. Mmmmm! Taking a large bite, I could feel my body relaxing into happiness. Okay, so I was consuming enough calories to fuel me for a month, but everyone knows that birthday pizza calories don't count!

'Mummy? Mummy?'

My reverie was interrupted by a very sorry sounding little voice. Frowning, I put down my pizza and looked around for my daughter. I couldn't see her anywhere. Had she found a hiding place she couldn't escape from?

'Grace? Where are you hiding?'

'I'm outside, Mummy.'

Outside?

A rush of panic flooded my body as I hurried to the door. Opening it, I saw my tiny daughter standing in front of me.

'I'm sorry, Mummy. I wanted to help you with the pizza.'

I scooped my daughter up in my arms and carried her inside for a huge cuddle.

'It's okay, baby.' I kissed the top of her head. 'You didn't do anything wrong. But let's play a different game now.'

Looking at the pizza lying on the table, my appetite had completely gone. How could I have missed Grace going outside? Anything could have happened to her. I was so focused on feeling sorry for myself that I'd dropped the ball. It might only have been for a moment, but things could have gone very wrong.

That's when I decided to go on a diet.

My friend Natalie had the opposite problem. A mum of twin girls, I always admired her svelte figure. I just had the one child and there I was stuffing my face with pizza and losing my child when the delivery guy comes, while she seemed to have it all together. She was a total supermum, looking gorgeous while effortlessly looking after her daughters – or so it seemed.

One time we met up for a coffee in a soft play area. After letting the children wear themselves out playing, we strapped them into highchairs in the café and took some much-deserved time out to catch up with each other.

'I don't know how you do it,' I told her. 'You look amazing! What's your secret? I could do with some dieting tips. I've given up pizza, but maybe you could let me have the details of your personal trainer…'

'I'm the last person to come to for diet advice.' Natalie sighed. 'You want to know the secret to my figure? I live off one biscuit a day because I just don't have time to eat properly.'

'You're kidding?'

'Nope.' Natalie shook her head sadly. 'And as for the gym, I haven't been since the girls were born. I get all my exercise from chasing them down all the time. It's like they instinctively know if they run in opposite directions, at least one of them is going to get away from me.'

'Wow.' I couldn't believe what I was hearing.

All this time I thought my friend had the perfect life and she was barely keeping her head above water, just like me.

'So which girl do you go after first?'

Natalie didn't even have to think about it. 'Rose.'

'Ahh.' I nodded sagely, sipping my coffee. 'She's your favourite.'

'No,' Natalie corrected me. 'She's the most fearless. If I don't go after Rose, she'll get herself into serious trouble. Rebecca only runs away because Rose is doing it. She gets bored pretty quickly, so I know she'll come back, where Rose would keep on going if I don't get to her first.'

That conversation was a real eye opener for me. I realised it doesn't matter whether you've gained weight after having kids and can't lose it, or the weight falls off you practically overnight. Becoming a mum changes you in ways that go way beyond just the physical. You're not the highest priority in your life anymore. You can't be. Your child has to come first all the time. And while that's a beautiful thing, it unfortunately often means that self-care gets put on the back burner or forgotten about all together because our days are filled with never-ending nappy changes and our nights are constantly interrupted.

If that sounds familiar, I've got a newsflash for you. Being a good parent does **not** mean your children should take over your life to the point where you become a shadow of your former self. You still need to prioritise time for yourself. Crucially, you should take a break on a regular basis to follow your own interests. And much as it might be tempting to use that time out to catch up on sleep, I strongly urge you to leave the napping and do something that brings you joy, something you enjoy doing and that helps you connect with the person you were before you had children and the person you are now that you're a parent.

Keep communication open with your partner so you can work as a family unit to support your needs as well as your child's. If you are a single parent, this might be difficult – trust me. I'm living it myself!

If you're sharing custody with your child's other parent, you can use the time they have with your child to do more than catch up with chores around the house. Make sure you schedule time to catch up with your friends. Don't be afraid to just spend a day binge watching Netflix if that's what you need to rest and recharge. It is absolutely okay to do nothing and not be on duty 24/7.

If, like me, your ex-partner isn't around, there are still options. If you have family, get them involved. If you can afford it, hire a babysitter. Alternatively, if you're on a budget, find other mums and swap babysitting duties with each other. Think creatively – it might feel like you haven't got anyone to help, but help is out there if you ask and hunt around.

I know it's easier said than done, but the earlier you can figure out a balance between looking after yourself and your children, the faster you will see an improvement in your overall health, happiness and wellbeing. Treat yourself as another one of your children! Be as kind and loving towards yourself as you are to them because you deserve love and understanding too. Be realistic about what you can and can't do – we often overestimate what we can do in a week but underestimate what we do in a year. I promise you, that first year of your child's life will go faster than any other year of your life and you'll look back and wonder how you managed to get through it – but you did, and you achieved so much more than you realised when you were knee deep in nappies and puree!

Whatever your personal situation, even if you're not able to get any help right now, the first step into incorporating self-care into your life is to be realistic about what you can and can't do.

Some days, all you're going to be capable of is making sure your child is fed and dressed. Trying to do all the chores as well is one step too far, so don't.

Give yourself permission to let the vacuum wait for another day. The world won't end. Letting your energies recover is the best possible thing you can do for yourself right now. Remember – parenting is so much easier when you're taking care of your own needs.

As a bare minimum, make sure you're meeting all your basic needs. Eat a healthy diet or if healthy is too much, then at least eat regularly! Then, as you get into the habit of regular meals, you can start improving the quality of what you eat. Get as much sleep as possible, and exercise. Don't worry about having a perfectly tidy home. As long as it's hygienic with clean bathrooms, fridges, etc. the rest is an added bonus that you don't have to stress about every day.

Take little steps. What often happens is people try to do too much too soon, get overwhelmed and give up on everything. Or you tell yourself you don't have time to spare for you – in which case you're more in need of self-care than you know!

So, instead of eating the kid's leftovers, make a point of eating a proper meal, and if the kids don't clean their plate, **don't** help them out by finishing it off. Eat with the children – it's much easier if you're all eating at the same time and it's a good habit to establish shared mealtimes at the table together.

Establish a sleep routine for yourself as well as for your children. I know that might sound strange, but if you're struggling with your sleep, everything else suffers. Sleep is one of the most important foundations for health. Give yourself a set bedtime, stop screen time at least an hour before you go to sleep and maybe listen to relaxing meditation music before you drift off.

Look at how you can build exercise in your day. If you can't follow along with a workout video on YouTube, and there are plenty of family friendly programs out there, then look at your day and think outside the box for your exercise. Can you walk somewhere with your child in a buggy or sling instead of driving? Can you take the stairs instead of the lift at work? Look at how you can be more active in your daily life until the time comes when you've got the time and opportunity to go to regular exercise classes.

If you're under an extreme amount of stress and anxiety, don't be afraid to consult a professional. There's no shame in getting support from a mental health professional if you're going through challenging times. If you'd broken a leg, you'd go to a doctor to help with the healing process, and our mental health is just as important as our physical.

Speaking of physical health, if you're finding yourself feeling down or tired with no obvious cause, it's possible that, just like me, there might be an actual physical issue causing your symptoms. It's always worth getting yourself checked out if you think there's something wrong. If there is a problem, you can come up with a solution and life becomes better.

Once you're ready to expand your self-care practice here's a few things you might like to incorporate:

- **Meditate.** There is ample research to show that meditation has a number of health benefits for mind, body and spirit. It can reduce stress[2] and stress related issues such as high blood pressure,[3] and even help you get a better night's sleep.[4] You can enjoy all these benefits with as little as five minutes' meditation a day. There are many guided meditations on YouTube to support you in getting started. I love Davidji's meditations,[5] but if he doesn't appeal to you, there are plenty of other options out there. If finding time is a problem for you, try meditating first thing in the morning before you get up or last thing at night before you go to sleep.

- **Go back to nature.** This is also supported by science – just 2 hours spent outside in nature every week has a positive impact on your mood and wellbeing.[6] Go for a walk in the park with the kids, let them play on the swings while you relax on a bench, or get out and garden. This is something you can do with the children – they love being outside too! If getting outdoors isn't possible for whatever reason, there is some evidence to suggest that looking at pictures of landscapes can also have a calming effect.[7]
- **Get dancing!** Putting on a positive, upbeat song and dancing around is a fast, effective way to lift your mood. The great thing about your children being your audience is they'll think you're the best dancer they've ever seen and it's so much fun being silly, dancing around and singing at the tops of your voice.

action steps

- Take a moment to examine your current lifestyle and identify all the ways in which you can take better care of yourself. You might like to journal on this. Consider your diet, exercise and sleep regime as a bare minimum and be brutally honest with yourself about how you're currently living.
- Once you have a snapshot of your current self-care practices, or lack thereof, list out ideas for how you can improve in the three basic areas of diet, exercise and sleep. Draw four columns on a piece of paper and brainstorm your ideas for what you can do in these three areas, as well as a fourth area – doing what brings you joy.
- Now you know all the things you could do to improve your life, pick **one** thing and make a commitment to doing it every day for a week. At the end of that week look back

and examine the positive impact it's made on your life and choose a second thing you can start doing. Slowly build up your self-care routine and make it absolutely non-negotiable. You cannot look after anyone else if you don't look after yourself first, so now's the time to start treating yourself the way you deserve.

- Look at yourself in the mirror and say out loud, 'I commit to properly taking care of myself each and every day!'
- If you think you may be struggling with parental burnout, please visit my website www.deborahbyrne.com to download a free eBook on how to overcome parental burnout.

CHAPTER TWO

where has the day gone?
going from time poor to time rich

Tomorrow – a mystical land where 99% of all human productivity, motivation and achievement is stored – Sir Ken Robinson

Do you ever try to recall what you used to do at the weekend before you had children? I look back now and I cannot for the life of me remember what I did with all those hours I had to play with before I had a child by my side demanding that I play with *her*.

I used to be a pretty laid-back person. Well, I still am, but where in the past it didn't matter whether someone was 10 minutes late or not, now I'm on Grace's schedule and she's nowhere near as understanding of anyone else's poor timekeeping.

In the past, if someone was 10 minutes late, I was all, 'It's cool! I can have an extra coffee while I'm waiting! I can catch up on emails! I can make a quick phone call!' Or even – gasp! – simply spend 10 minutes chilling.

Now I've got Grace with me, if someone's late, there's a good chance I won't be able to wait for them. Grace might decide she doesn't like the colour of the drink she was so desperate for 5 minutes earlier and throw a tantrum. She might have chewed through all the snacks I brought with me (literally!) and is now turning her attention on how she can destroy the café to entertain herself. Hurricane Grace strikes again!

It's amazing how much devastation a 2-year-old can cause in a short space of time and I know my daughter well enough to spot the warning signs and head off trouble before it starts. Unfortunately, if that means I can't keep waiting for you, you're out of luck and we're going to have to find another toddler-friendly window to catch up. Believe me, I'd much rather rearrange than have to explain – again – that my daughter is lovely really and doesn't normally try to shoplift all the sweets from the café's cookie jar.

The reality is that young children have absolutely no concept of time. They inhabit a completely different world to us, one that I'd love to go back to sometimes. They think nothing of stopping dead in their tracks to stare at a dead bug they've spotted on the ground. They don't care that you've only got a few seconds left before the traffic lights turn green and you're going to be hit with a barrage of car horns telling you to get out of the way while you wrangle a screaming child desperate to give that dead bug an appropriate funeral, complete with hearse and mourners.

Their ability to live in the moment is a truly beautiful thing and it's an ability so many adults work incredibly hard to cultivate. But going from adult time to kid time can be a real culture shock. Children don't understand the urgency of deadlines or why it's so important to be at the doctors in plenty of time for your appointment. They just want to do whatever they want to do **right now!** If only we parents had that same luxury.

A friend of mine, Becky, was working from home during lockdown and getting to grips with having meetings on Zoom instead of in person with children running around in the background. She had two young boys aged 6 and 4, old enough to occupy themselves for short bursts of time but not so old that she could rely on them entertaining themselves if she hadn't sorted something out in advance.

Becky had a major pitch scheduled with an important new client. She needed the boys to be quiet during the meeting, so she got organised. She signed up to Disney+ so her children could watch the latest Disney film (or more likely *Frozen* for the gazillionth time. Just let it go already!) but she didn't tell them about it until just before she went into her meeting. She spent time one-on-one with the boys before the meeting so they'd had plenty of her time and attention. They'd baked cookies and Becky had it all timed so perfectly that she was able to sit the boys down with cookies fresh out of the oven in front of their movie of choice. (Yep, you guessed it – *Frozen*!) She was perfectly on time to log into Zoom and she plastered on her biggest, brightest smile to impress her potential new client.

It was only when the camera came on that she realised she was still wearing the cookie dough smeared old T shirt she'd thrown on to play with the boys! Becky had been so caught up in making sure the boys were ready for her meeting, she'd completely lost track of time and forgot to get *herself* ready.

Fortunately, the client saw the funny side and was impressed enough by her pitch to hire her anyway, but Becky promised herself she would remember to organise herself, as well as everyone else, next time.

It's so easy to lose yourself in your children and get overwhelmed with all the tasks you've got to get done in the day. In fact, research has shown we spend far more time with our children than our parents ever did with us. A University of Maryland study found that for 3- to 11-year-olds, mothers spend an average of 11 to 30 hours each week, either fully engaged in activities with their kids, or at least nearby and available when needed.

It didn't get much better as their children grew – for kids in their early teens, mums are there between 11 and 20 hours each week. In comparison, on average, in 1975 mums spent just over 7 hours per week with their kids.[8]

Newsflash – your children don't need you to be a helicopter parent! It's absolutely okay to leave them to their own devices in an age-appropriate way. And once you recognise you're allowed to spend less time with your children, it opens up a whole new world of possibilities.

If there's one problem I've seen over and over again with all the families I've worked with, it's the issue of how to find enough time in the day to get everything done. The truth is you don't necessarily **have** to do everything. Once you recognise that and release your attachment to trying to do "All The Things", you immediately feel lighter because you're free of that burden. I know it was a real eye opener for me to see that, while there are still plenty of things you've got to get done as a parent, there's an awful lot we do because we think we "should", which really don't help anyone. Clearing out your to-do list and organising your time will make a huge difference to your life.

There are three main fundamental pillars of time you need to devote your attention to:

1. **Your career.** Whatever you do, you should know how many hours per week you spend on your career. This is non-negotiable (unless and until you change jobs). If you're launching a business or working towards a promotion, you may even need to spend more time than average at work.
2. **Your relationships.** This includes your relationship with your partner as well as your children. If you've got regular commitments like swimming lessons or dance classes, you'll know that you need to mark out that time, but you should also decide on how much time you want to actively devote to your family relationships.

3. **Yourself.** Yep, you need to reserve a certain amount of time for yourself to relax, recharge and recuperate, just as we discussed in the first chapter.

What tends to happen is parents cut back on the amount of time they spend on the third pillar so they can get everything else done. They think they can sacrifice this time for themselves and somehow make it up later – but they never do.

Let's be real. There are 168 hours in a week. That's a fixed amount. It doesn't matter what magic you weave – you'll never get more than 24 hours in a day. That's why it's so important to prioritise the most important and let go of everything else.

There's a TedTalk by Laura Vanderkam[9] I think every parent should watch. It breaks down why time management is so important and outlines what you can do to make more time for yourself. For example, she talks about how people watch a television show and think they can get other tasks done during the ad breaks or even multitasking while they watch. But, as Laura says, an even better way to make more time is to not watch the show in the first place!

It's not a long talk, but it's a real eye opener. I strongly recommend you go watch it right now before you read any further. You'll find the link in the reference section at the end of this book.

If you're not convinced yet about the importance of time management, here's 10 reasons why you need to get control of your time:

1. **It makes you more self-disciplined.** If you're able to manage your time, the chances are high you can manage other aspects of your life, even if you can't see it right now. Someone who is self-disciplined knows how to fight through procrastination to achieve their goals. Self-discipline is one of the most important skills when it comes to being successful in life and the great thing is,

it's a skill you can learn. No more telling yourself you're useless with time – you've got everything you need to get everything done and more.

4. **It makes you more productive.** Once you've sorted out how to manage your time, you can say goodbye to those late nights trying to finish up your to-do list. You get to spend more time doing the things you need – having romantic date nights with your partner or simply getting to bed on time. Over a third of American adults don't get a good night's sleep,[10] which impacts on their ability to function in their daily lives. Managing your time so you can get enough rest has countless positive benefits.

5. **It allows you to relax.** The whole of the first chapter was devoted to the importance of self-care. You can't look after yourself if you don't think you have enough time. When you start organising your time, you can incorporate down time so you can properly relax after a long day and prepare yourself for doing it all over again tomorrow.

6. **It lowers stress.** A lot of this book covers how you can lower stress, which is such a huge problem for so many parents. If you feel like your time isn't your own and you're constantly playing catchup with deadlines, I can guarantee your health will be suffering as a consequence. Once you get a handle on your time, you'll find a lot of the burden, caused by poor time management, falls away, making you more productive and more relaxed by default.

7. **It opens new doors.** When you're constantly rushing from one task to the next, there's no space in your life to try anything new. You might want to sign up for a belly dance class or just read a book but with your schedule? Forget about it! Once you've got your diary under control, you've got more time for your children and more

time for yourself. Parents often talk about losing who they are because of their children. I know, I felt that way for a while. When you have more time, you can start doing those things you've always wanted to do but kept putting off.

8. **It makes your relationships better.** It's a no brainer really. When you've got more time to spend with friends and family, the closer your bonds will be. Not only that, but you'll be happier because you've got the time for what's really important in life. Your whole life improves when your relationships improve.

9. **It helps your career.** Strong time management means you're making time for yourself. You're getting the rest and sleep you need to ensure you're functioning at your best. When you're at your best, by default your performance improves at work, which makes it easier for you to make a good impression on the right people to further your career.

10. **It makes you a better decision maker.** You can't think straight if your brain is foggy from lack of sleep and overwhelm. When you lower stress and increase sleep by managing your time, this has a major effect on your ability to make good decisions in all aspects of your life. When you're stressed and time poor, you find yourself saying yes to your child when they ask for that cookie, even though you know you should say no. Anything to avoid the tantrum you just haven't got the ability to deal with! When you reduce that stress and give yourself more time, you have the strength to say no and weather the ensuing tantrum, so your child understands you have firm boundaries.

11. **You get more done.** There's a saying – do less to do more. Believe it or not, you get way more done when

you don't feel like you're always playing catchup. You're not juggling multiple tasks, incapable of giving enough time to any of them. Instead, you get one thing done then another and before you know it, you've had a wonderfully productive day and you're all geared up for doing the same tomorrow.

12. **You take advantage of opportunities.** By now, you should be able to see that poor time management drastically reduces your productivity. This will cost you valuable opportunities. If a childless colleague is outperforming you, the chances are high they'll be promoted over you – frustrating or what? If you want to keep up with your peers *and* bring in all the valuable skills your parenting experience has given you, good time management will help you prioritise your time, opening unexpected opportunities for you – and allowing you to make the most of them. Likewise, if you can get everything done at work, you can leave it behind you at the end of the day, leaving weekends and evenings free for you to spend more time with your family and friends.

the four ds funnel system

The Four Ds Funnel System is one of my absolute favourite time management systems. It's so simple and yet so powerful. When you use it, you can immediately place a task in its appropriate context and prioritise it accordingly. I'll be honest – when I first discovered the Four Ds, I started using it **all the time**! I got such a kick out of deciding where a particular task fit on the spectrum that it automatically made those annoying chores way more fun because I'd funnelled them appropriately.

The Four Ds are as follows:
- **Do:** Important and urgent.

- **Delete:** Not important, not urgent.
- **Delay:** Important but not urgent.
- **Delegate:** Not important but urgent.

That's it. When a task comes up, all you have to do is ask yourself, 'Is this important? Is this urgent?'

If it's both, then you know you need to get it done – stat! So if your child comes up to you doing that familiar little dance, jogging from one foot to the other as they wail, 'Mummy! I need a wee!!' you don't even have to ask – it's important and urgent! You stop what you're doing and you get it done. Whereas if they come up to you, tablet in hand and say, 'Mummy! Watch this video of a cat doing a funny dance!' it's not important and not urgent, so it's absolutely okay to say, 'No thank you,' if you're right in the middle of doing something else.

As part of your commitment to improving your time management, you might decide that you're going to spend 15 minutes at the end of the day listing out your must-do tasks for the next day. It's an important task but not urgent, so it can wait until after you've got the kids ready for bed, read them their stories and put your feet up for a bit.

This is the kind of task you'll find yourself automating, building it into your routine so it becomes as normal as brushing your teeth or getting dressed in the morning. Conversely, your child coming up to you every 5 minutes wanting your attention isn't important in the slightest, but experience has taught you that it's urgent for you to attend to their needs, otherwise they might escalate ways to get you to spend time with them.

This is when it's time to delegate. If there's someone else who can tackle what they need, do that before it moves into the important and urgent box. Alternatively, look at what you're currently doing – if you're answering emails or dealing with phone calls, it's possible someone else can do that task for you. If you're self-employed, for example, a VA (virtual assistant) can do many of those mundane jobs, freeing your time for more important, urgent tasks.

action steps

- Watch the Laura Vanderkam TedTalk. (Details are in the references section at the end of this book.) Make sure you take notes and think about how you can apply the principles she discusses to your own life.
- Recognise you have more time than you think. Sit down with your schedule (you might like to get a large family planner for this task) and start assigning time to the three pillars according to the needs you identified earlier in this chapter. Block out your work time as a non-negotiable and then do the same for any regular activities you and your children have. Now decide on how much time you want to give to your partner if you have one. Give at least the same amount of time to yourself. Mark these in your calendar and treat them as meetings as important as any you have for work. Look at how much time you have left over – and resist the temptation to fill it with other tasks! Allow yourself room to breathe and over-estimate the amount of time you'll need for anything, so you don't end up feeling rushed.
- Start using the Four Ds Funnel System to delegate your tasks appropriately. You can apply this to jobs around the house as effectively as you can anything at work. This might give you the push you need to finally budget for a cleaner. Imagine delegating all the household chores. Bliss!
- Visit my website www.deborahbyrne.com and sign up to my free webinar where I'll give you some of my best productivity hacks for parents with busy schedules. In the webinar I go deeper into the subject of time management

so you can have the confidence of knowing yes, you *do* have time to get everything done and yes, you *can* get organised, even with small children about the place.

CHAPTER THREE

your family personalities –
i'm related to people i don't relate to!

The most important thing you wear is your personality
– America Ferrara

I have a friend, we'll call her Jayne, who has 5 daughters aged between 9 and 3. Four of her children look like their father – dark hair, dark eyes, athletic build. But one of them couldn't be more opposite. Sonja has blonde hair and blue eyes and is incredibly petite. Whenever Jayne is out with them, she always gets people asking if she's a childminder because the children are so close in age, and she has so many.

When Jayne replies they're all hers, the next question is whether Sonja is adopted. Pretty rude, huh? But that's not the worst of it. Jayne has even had people suggest her daughter was switched at the hospital! Fortunately, she knows that's impossible since Sonja was born on her front room floor. But can you imagine having children who look so different, strangers think they can comment on their possible origins?

It's not just that Sonja looks different to her siblings either. Her closest sister, Kayla, couldn't be more polar opposite when it comes to personality. Sonja loves rules – Kayla loves to smash them to smithereens! Sonja takes pride in being well behaved and polite – Kayla once told her mum, 'I like being naughty because it's fun!' Their differences even go so far with Sonja being left-handed and Kayla right-handed.

Every time I see Jayne's family, it never ceases to amaze me how genetics can have such different results. I'm stunned she doesn't have more grey hair. Parenting 5 kids is challenging enough for anyone, but having children with such wildly differing needs adds an extra layer of "fun" for Jayne.

Fortunately for Jayne, she's the kind of person who takes everything in her stride. She makes it look easy while I'm having days wondering how she can deal with 5 when my sole child is pushing the boundaries and all my buttons.

It hasn't been so easy for a client of mine, Alison. I've known her for years, but she only came to me for help recently. She's one of those people who's got so much love to give. She's always been generous with her time and affection. She'd do anything to help anyone in need and I consider myself very lucky to know her.

So, it was a surprise when she hired me as a coach. All I'd ever heard was what a great mum she was. We went out on a play date with our children (she's got a little girl, Hunter, not much older than my Grace and a 5-year-old son called Hayden) and I was struck by how affectionate they were with her. They'd often come running up to her just so they could give her a hug. From the outside it looked like the perfect setup.

But as we pushed our daughters on the swings, Alison confided in me that although she didn't doubt her children loved her, she didn't feel like they respected her. I said nothing, just listened as she told me about how her children were difficult to manage.

They wouldn't go to bed when she asked and she was worn out from the lack of sleep.

'I thought sleepless nights would stop once the kids were out of nappies, Deborah,' she said. 'Instead, they've got me chasing them round the house, trying to get them to stay in bed. It's even worse than when they were babies!'

When it was time for us to leave the playground, I started to see why her children were the ones in charge. When I told Grace it was time to leave, although she pouted a little, she took my hand and was happy for me to lead the way back to the car.

Hayden and Hunter on the other hand. When Alison first told them it was time to go, they ignored her. When she repeated herself, Hunter said, 'No, Mummy. We're playing a game. I'm the princess and Hayden's the dragon. We have to finish the game first.'

'Okay,' Alison replied. 'You can have 5 more minutes, but that's it, okay? We have to go home and get lunch.'

I said nothing as I strapped Grace into her car seat. I heard Alison calling her children to get in the car. I also heard them laugh as they carried on playing.

'Do you see what I mean?' asked Alison in exasperation, coming over to me for help while her kids continued to play. 'They just don't listen to me. I don't understand it. They keep telling me they love me, so why do they treat me like this?'

'Let's go into that in our next coaching session,' I suggested as I called to her kids to leave the playground. Immediately, they stopped what they were doing and ran over to their mum's car.

'How do you do that?' Alison gasped.

'Magic.' I tapped the side of my nose. 'But don't worry – I'll teach you the spell when we meet.'

The reality was Alison was a permissive parent, letting her children do whatever they wanted without setting and maintaining firm boundaries. Fortunately, I was able to give her a number of techniques to use with her children and, although it took time and work, Alison started to put boundaries in place and earn the respect of her children – who still loved her as much as they did back when she was a pushover.

Two of my clients, Mike and Caroline, decided they wanted to start having a weekly house clean with all the children. Their two kids were 9 and 6 years old, so old enough to be able to help out with the chores. Caroline had told me she was fed up with being expected to do the lion's share of the cleaning, so this was a solution we'd come up to teach the children some responsibility while relieving some of the pressure on Caroline.

Max, their 9-year-old, was tasked with mopping the floor. When Mike went in to check his son's progress, he wasn't impressed.

'Come on, lad! Put some elbow grease into it!' he said and went off to see how his daughter was doing.

Coming back half an hour later, he was annoyed to see Max hadn't done any more mopping. Instead, he was rooting around in the cupboards.

'What's the problem?' he said, trying to keep his temper under control. 'You should be finished by now. Come on, Max. The sooner you get this finished, the more time you've got to play.'

'But, Dad,' Max wailed, 'I can't find the elbow grease.'

Before we have children, we tend to assume we're going to give birth to mini-mes, a miniature version of yourself who likes the same things we do, has the same personality traits and will be really easy to relate to because they think just like you! It can be quite a culture shock when you meet your child and discover they're a person in their own right.

Maybe they're like you, but maybe they're the complete opposite. After all, your child has two parents, so there's no guarantee they'll have your personality traits instead of your partner's. Or they do take after you, but in the areas you don't like or aren't even aware you have. Or you and your partner both have a certain personality trait, such as stubbornness, and your child gets a double dose of it. So, they're like you, only turned up to 10! This is what happened to a couple I know and when they disagree on something, they *really* clash.

Knowing your personality type and that of your children is one of the best parenting tools you can have in your toolkit. When you know the best way to approach your child, it becomes much easier for you to communicate effectively with them. You can talk in a way that means they'll genuinely listen to you and understand what you're saying. Likewise, when you know your own personality, you can appreciate how that impacts on the way you communicate with those around you and react in any given situation. Everyone benefits when you take the time out to understand yourself and your child better.

There are a number of different ways in which various personality types can be categorised. Most people have heard of the Myers-Briggs scale, which places people in 1 of 16 groups based on whether they have one or the other of four basic personality traits – extrovert/introvert, sensing/intuition, thinking/feeling and judging/perceiving.

Extroverts thrive on the energy they get from being around and interacting with others, while introverts recharge by themselves in quiet reflection. Sensing people learn best when information is given in a detailed, sequential manner while intuitives learn better when the emphasis is more on the meaning and associations between different pieces of information. Thinking types are mainly driven by logic and use deductive reasoning to come to conclusions, while feeling types are more emotion led, who personalise issues and causes and consider other people's perspectives. Judging people like information to be organised and structured, while perceiving individuals do best in a flexible learning environment filled with new, interesting ideas.

This way of identifying personality types can be useful when supporting your child. While Myers-Briggs is an excellent assessment tool used globally for a variety of reasons, I personally prefer to use the DISC scale to sort personality traits.

DISC is simpler because it only considers 4 main personality types:

- **Dominance.** These are very forceful individuals who are natural leaders, although they can sometimes come across as domineering and bossy. They aren't shy about coming forward and are happy to speak their mind. They make up their minds quickly and go for what they want the moment they know what that is.
- **Influence.** These people love being in the middle of the action, whatever it might be. They thrive on attention, love to feel admired and want to be applauded for their efforts. They need to be seen for who they are and know they are highly valued.
- **Steadiness.** These are the people-oriented individuals, the ones who need lots of close, friendly relationships in order to feel secure. They can veer into people pleasing because they love harmonious relationships and hate seeing others upset.
- **Conscientiousness.** These are the hard workers of the group. They are analytical and highly independent, happy to work on their own. It is important to them for things to be correct. They need their world to be organised and to know what is expected of them so they can get on with doing it.

There are a number of reasons why I prefer using DISC[11] with the families I work with. Myers-Briggs tends to take the view that your personality is fixed and rarely changes. DISC understands that individuals can behave differently in different circumstances. So while your child might be a model of good behaviour at school, working hard and getting good grades, at home they might be messy and need a lot more encouragement to help out with the chores. Myers-Briggs gives you an idea of how you tick on the inside; DISC looks at how your personality manifests itself in your behaviour, which is invaluable to any parent looking to understand their child better.

Myers-Briggs results can be difficult to remember. I've done online tests multiple times because I keep forgetting my answer, whereas, since DISC is a more straightforward system, it's easier to remember what type you and your child are. It's much easier to implement what you learn from a DISC assessment. You can even explain it to your children – you can often represent your DISC results in a circular or quadrant diagram that can be understood at a glance.

DISC allows you to understand yourself better but also gives you a structure for understanding and relating to others. With Myers-Briggs, in order for it to be most effective, you'd need to know which personality type your children are so you can then work out the best way for you to interact. Myers-Briggs test can take a very long time, which means if your child is young, they're unlikely to be able to sit through all the questions. DISC enables you to get to know your child's type very quickly and you can put it into practice straightaway, regardless of whether your child is aware of their type or not.

I like to use four animals to represent the four different DISC types: Panther for dominance, peacock for influence, dolphin for steadiness and owl for conscientiousness. Before reading on, I highly recommend you find an online quiz and determine which of the four personalities fits you.

I want you to remember that there's no good or bad, right or wrong when it comes to personality types. There's strengths and weaknesses to each of them. This is an exercise in understanding so you can communicate more effectively. Communication is the most important skill you can have if you're looking to elevate your family relationships.

Here's a brief summary of each of the four personality types:

panther

Panthers are very action-oriented and decisive. They are natural problem solvers and highly assertive, although this assertiveness can border on aggression. They are adventurous and independent, but they can also be very demanding of those around them.

Panthers value, and are motivated by, challenges. They love feeling like they have power and authority and need to be given options rather than told what to do.

peacock

Peacocks love to talk! Outgoing and enthusiastic, they are highly charming and animated in how they interact with others. They can be very emotional. They are optimistic and generous with their time and possessions. Their love of language makes them very persuasive and engaging – these are the children who can wrap their parents round their little finger. Peacocks value, and are motivated by, social recognition. They love to be with people, providing service and engaging in group activities.

dolphin

Dolphins are patient and loyal. They can seem wise beyond their years, so try to remember they are still just children. They're team players who will go along with what the group wants to make everyone happy. They are gentle and empathetic, trusting of those around them, but they love to ask why. Dolphins value, and are motivated by, guarantees and security. They need to feel appreciated and quality control is important to them.

owl

Owls are the diplomats of the family. They are conventional – these are not people who like to stand out. The truth matters to them, so they'll go out of their way to find the facts of the matter. Diplomatic and deliberate, owls are precise and analytical in everything they do. They make decisions based in logic rather than emotion and can be cautious when dealing with others or new situations. Owls value, and are motivated by, tradition. They have high standards and pay close attention to detail. They love everything to be perfect.

Each animal seeks validation and approval from others in different ways. Panthers get validation from results and like it when people listen to their instructions. Peacocks get validation from recognition and like to check for appropriate behaviour. Dolphins get validation from security and like to initiate relationships. Owls get validation from being correct and like making decisions.

Given all of this, think about what animal most closely fits your child. Are they a self-confident panther? A people loving dolphin? A perfectionist owl? It's very common to have more than one animal in your family that can make for... um... *interesting* times.

Picture the scene: you're a dolphin with two children, a panther and a peacock. You want the children to go to bed at 8 p.m. on a school night. Every evening you find yourself struggling to get them into bed. The panther wants to be in control of every little aspect of the bedtime routine, from choosing their pyjamas, to picking the bedtime story, to negotiating for just 5 minutes more. As a people pleasing dolphin, you find yourself giving in to your panther's demands, struggling to get them to settle down much before 8.30 p.m.

And that's before you've had a chance to deal with your

peacock. You think the peacock will be easy in comparison, but they insist on talking over every little thing that's happened that day. You want them to be happy, so you smile and nod as they prattle away, but it's another half hour before you can finally kiss them goodnight. It's a rare evening you get them in bed before 9 p.m. and often your panther gets up again to ask you for a glass of water or the peacock comes to tell you why they can't sleep.

Two completely different reactions and a parent who feels completely out of their depth because they don't know how to communicate effectively with their children's animal. The more you can communicate in a way that speaks directly to their animal, the better your relationship with be.

effective communication with the four animal types

With panthers, you should always be specific, clear and brief. Give them choice (but not too much choice) so they can feel like they're in control. Provide them with facts and figures and remember they are motivated by results and goals. Support their results as much as possible and let them feel like they're in charge of their life as much as possible. Do not ramble or waste their time – they hate that! Be clear rather than cloudy, but do not give them orders. Once you've told them what you want them to do, don't add any epilogues or extra conditions. Save that for later.

If you have a little peacock in your family, leave plenty of time for socialising. Talk about people and their goals and always ask for your peacock's opinion. Give them plenty of ideas and plan fun activities together. Don't be too direct or cold and avoid focusing on facts and figures. It's a waste of time being task-oriented, so don't stick to your agenda too much. Dolphins hate being talked down to or having to wait for a decision, so always keep that in mind when you're dealing with them.

If your child is a dolphin, make sure you clearly define personal contributions. Be genuinely interested in them and the things they love and avoid being threatening in your interactions. Ask them plenty of "how' questions" and listen carefully to the answer. Don't try to rush into things – give your dolphin plenty of notice – and don't be demanding. Attempting to debate facts and figures is a waste of time with a dolphin, so don't bother. They hate vagueness and don't like to feel rushed into responding.

If you have an owl in your family, take your time with them and prepare your discussions in advance. Be direct and give them tangible, practical evidence for what you want them to do. Give them plenty of guarantees and be ready to go into the pros and cons. Don't be disorganised or too casual and don't try to give them personal incentives – they won't work. Owls prize punctuality, but they like to take their time when it comes to making a decision, so don't rush them. Be true to yourself rather than using someone else's opinion to sway them.

Always remember that ultimately we're all individuals and our personalities can change with time and circumstances, so don't be too rigid when using these personality types. A peacock might display dolphin traits when they're on a playdate or an owl could be more panther-like when placed in a group, so take these personality types as a guide you can return to time and again as your child grows to ensure you're still communicating in a way that best suits them. If you want to get the most out of your relationship with your child, it's important to appreciate what they value and what motivates them. There's no right or wrong when it comes to communication. We're all just people with our own personal preferences.

action steps

- Find a DISC quiz and do it to discover your personality type.
- Either get your child to do the quiz or, if they're too young or aren't interested, do it on their behalf to see what their personality type is.
- Use the section on effective communication to guide how you communicate with your children and other important people in your life.

CHAPTER FOUR

your emotional tool kit – is it wine o'clock yet?

When dealing with people, remember you are not dealing with creatures of logic, but creatures of emotion – Dale Carnegie

I remember my dad told me a joke once and it seems appropriate to share it with you to introduce this chapter.

A girl had to write an essay for homework, and she asked her dad if he'd help her.

'Sure,' her father said. 'What are you writing about?'

'The difference between anger and exasperation. I can't seem to explain it.'

'I see.' Her dad nodded. 'They are very similar. But there is a difference – it's all a matter of degree. It's probably easier to show you than explain it.'

He picked up his phone and dialled a random number. When a man replied, the girl's dad said, 'Hello. Is Curt there?'

'Wrong number,' came the short reply as the other person hung up.

The girl's dad gave her a knowing glance as he redialled the number.

'Hello. Is Curt there?'

'I told you before,' snapped the man on the other end of the line, 'you've got a wrong number. Why don't you check the number before you dial?'

'Can you see how that man's getting angry?' the girl's father said. 'He's going about his day, and here we are, interrupting him to ask for someone we know isn't there.'

Once again, he rang the number.

'Hello. Is Curt there?'

'Listen, pal,' yelled the man on the other end of the line. 'I told you there's no Curt here. Stop dialling my number!' He slammed the phone down hard.

'Okay,' the father said to his daughter. 'So you know what anger is now, right?'

'Yes.' The girl nodded.

'Time for exasperation.' Once more, the father rang the number.

A very angry voice replied, 'Yes?'

'Hello,' said the father. 'This is Curt. Have there been any calls for me..?'

It might be a joke, but for many of us, this is what it's like living with small children. We get asked the same question over and over and just when we think they're tired of asking, they ask all over again! No wonder I've got so many grey hairs when I look in the mirror.

But it's not just adults who can lose their temper over silly things. Children can get upset and overwhelmed too and at seemingly inconsequential matters. I remember giving Grace one of her favourite snack bars. She absolutely lost it because I'd had the temerity to open the packaging for her. I ended up taping it back together so she could open it for herself. I completely understand how important independence is to little ones but given that she'd gotten all upset last time I'd given her a snack bar because she couldn't open it, I thought I was being helpful.

There was another time when I offered Grace a packet of crisp chips. She was very emphatic that she didn't want any of the chips, chips were horrid, chips were the worst food in the world, so I ate the pack instead. At which point she burst into floods of tears because I'd eaten her chips. Sometimes you just can't win!

I really felt for my friend, Claire, though. She was driving cross country to visit family and was in the car with her two daughters for hours. Her oldest, Olivia, is 8 and she's a past master at winding up her younger sister Emma, who's 5. They hadn't been driving for long when Emma started crying. Olivia was looking out of "her" window and wouldn't stop. It didn't seem to matter how much Claire reasoned with her that you really can't control which window someone looks out of, Emma was absolutely insistent that Olivia should be banned from looking at the view on her side of the car. I don't know how Claire survived that journey with her sanity intact – she has the patience of a saint. She did confide in me there were times when the kids weren't the only ones yelling.

We all hit those moments when our internal cup of emotions gets full to overflowing. When your child asks 'why?' for the gazillionth time that day or you get a call from the school about your teen skipping class yet again, it takes all you've got not to scream at the top of your voice that you just want the world to stop so you can get off.

Parental stress is a serious problem for many of us. It strikes when there's a difference between the demands placed on you by your children and your available resources. If there's a deficit in your time, energy, patience, etc. stress can have a negative impact on your ability to parent effectively. If you don't do something about it, that stress can even result in physical symptoms like shoulder, neck or back pain, headaches or teeth grinding.

Your mental health also suffers when you're under too much stress. A lack of support or coping strategies can result in that stress developing into full blown parental burnout. That's where I found myself after Grace was born and it's a feeling I never want to experience again.

Some of us are better at coping with stress than others and we all have different reactions when we feel under pressure. The more you are made aware of your own limits and triggers, the more effective your coping strategies will be.

Triggers are events that activate your brain's amygdala, resulting in difficult emotions or psychological symptoms, such as anxiety, negativity, despair or feeling like a failure. We all have things that trigger us and most of the time, our reactions to them are a normal part of human psychology. However, if you are unaware of your triggers and don't deal with them appropriately, you can find yourself suffering from parental burnout and other mental health conditions. This is why it's so important to identify your triggers and decide on the best way to deal with them.

Knowledge is power. The first step is to recognise the cause of your triggers. Once you've done that, you can analyse them and be more conscious in your reaction when you are triggered.

For example, it might be that your children are always arguing over their toys, and you struggle to deal with it calmly. Instead, you find yourself yelling at them to just share already. If you take a step back and reflect on why this is, you might remember that when you were a child, you wanted to play with your big brother's toys, but you were never allowed. It's hard for you to see your children following the same pattern when you had visions of them happily sharing their toys and having lots of fun together.

Looking at this rationally, you need to take yourself out of the equation. Your children are not you and their experiences are not yours. Instead, ask why it is your children are having problems sharing. Make a point of talking to each of them separately at a time when you're all feeling calm to discover what's really going on. Then next time you feel yourself being triggered by your children's behaviours, recognise your own emotional state and take a moment to breathe to calm yourself down. Then recognise and acknowledge your children's feelings before responding to them rationally.

You may not remember everything about your childhood, but there are a number of common triggers that parents can suffer from, not all of which are to do with your childhood. These can include:

- The anniversary of a loss or trauma
- Having too much on your to do list
- Relationships ending
- Being alone too much
- Feeling judged or criticised
- Financial pressures
- Physical illnesses
- Yelling
- Specific smells, tastes or noises.

Parenting is stressful enough without throwing triggers into the mix. Stress makes us more emotional, less patient and more frustrated, which in turn has an impact on our ability to respond rationally. Identifying your triggers means you can recognise stressful situations right from the start so you can immediately begin managing your reactions.

Breathing and counting to 10 is a good start. Another good technique is to understand that when you feel stressed, this emotional state isn't permanent. When you name and accept your feelings just as they are and let them pass without judgement, they flow through you that much faster.

So, the next time you're feeling stressed, remember to let it RAIN:

- Recognise the state of mind you're experiencing.
- Accept and acknowledge the current situation.

- Investigate why you're feeling like this and ask what will happen if you continue to feel this way.
- Non-identify with your emotion. Your emotions are not you and you can let them pass.

There are a number of ways in which you can support yourself to cope more effectively with stress and stay cool under pressure:

- **Move your body.** We all know exercise is good for you. Staying active helps regulate your hormones and manage your stress. If you feel you haven't got time to hit the gym or go to a class, get moving with the kids. They'll love dancing around with you if you stick some music on or go for a bike ride together.
- **Get good quality sleep for 7 to 8 hours every night.** If stress is keeping you awake, look at ways of eliminating the cause. If your child is waking up at night, look to take turns with your partner, if you have one, so you can get rest every other night or get a babysitter in so you can have a good nap during the day. If money is a problem, look at speaking to a financial adviser or Citizen's Advice. If your relationship is going through a rough patch, consider having counselling. The great thing with sleep is it doesn't take much for you to catch up on it but neglecting it will make it so much harder for you to deal with your stress.
- **Eat well and limit your alcohol intake.** It's very tempting to unwind with a glass of wine at the end of a stressful day, but alcohol inhibits your body's ability to regulate its stress hormones, so keep it as an infrequent treat. Avoid processed foods and choose the healthy option as much as possible. Nourishing your body will work wonders for your ability to cope with stress.
- **Meditate or do yoga.** These relaxation techniques have been proven to lower the impact of stress on the body

as well as make it easier for you to stay calm in trying situations. Just a few minutes every day will have a positive effect. Look for meditation classes in your area, online or find YouTube videos to meditate with.
- **Get back to your hobbies.** It's very easy to lose sight of the things that bring us joy once children come into our lives. Start doing the things you used to love doing or start doing something that intrigues you. Many of these can involve your children, such as gardening or cooking, but you can also listen to music or curl up with a good book. Whatever you do, making time for activities you enjoy can decrease stress levels as well as lower your heart rate.[12]
- **Breathe.** Our breathing changes when we become stressed, so if you notice this happening, consciously start controlling your breath. Inhale deeply, hold for a moment, then slowly release. Slow breathing is one of the best natural stress relievers.

With the best will in the world, all the stress busting techniques still won't stop you having one of those days. Keeping your cool in the face of a determined child is enough to test the patience of a saint and we'll all have times when we're less than our best. When this happens, be kind to yourself. Beating yourself up won't change anything but it will make you feel worse, and nobody needs that. It'll only start you on a downward spiral.

When this happens, remind yourself that you are doing the hardest job in the world bringing up the next generation. Be proud of how much you've accomplished and look at your challenges as opportunities to learn rather than failures.

using your reticular activating system (ras) to combat stress

I want to share with you one very important tool you have with you right now that can help you completely shift the way you view the people around you. This is your Reticular Activating System, or RAS.

Have you ever said to your child, 'Don't drop that!' only for them to immediately smash the glass they're carrying? You're filled with 'I told you so's but really, it's your RAS talking.

The RAS is that part of your brain that looks for information to validate your existing beliefs. It filters the world through the lens you hold up to it, which is a summary of your experiences and beliefs. As Henry Ford said, 'Whether you think you can, or whether you think you can't, you're right.'

If you think you're bad at something, you're never going to get better at it. If you think you're good at something, you won't allow yourself to fail – and all of that is supported by your RAS. Your RAS enables you to see what you want to see and **only** what you want to see, which then influences your actions.

Your brain is an incredibly complex machine. It sifts through billions of pieces of data every moment, which can be overwhelming. That's why the RAS is such an important part of the brain. It filters out any unnecessary information so only the important stuff comes through.

Your RAS is the reason why you can be in a room full of noisy chatter, but if someone says your name or something sounding like it, you immediately hear and react. Your RAS system has been subconsciously programming your brain your whole life to take what you focus on and creates a filter for it, working on your behalf without you having to actively tell it to.

However, although this process is usually subconscious, it

is possible to train your RAS to filter in a way that suits you best. If you want to be more positive and enjoy a better outlook, teaching your RAS to focus on the good things will bring more of these into your life. So, for example, your child has just pulled all the wet wipes out of the package and left them all over the floor. If you were being negative, your reaction might be, 'My child always makes a mess!' Instead, turn this into a positive response by saying, 'My child is so curious about the world around them,' and then get your child to help you clean up.

The reason why reprogramming your RAS is so important is when you receive information, it is sent to your RAS, which filters it out using a process called sensory gating. Not all information is sent to be processed, most notably information that contradicts your world view. This means your RAS is constantly keeping your attention focused on information you already have, reinforcing your beliefs and making it easier for you to process and understand the world around you.

So, if you think your children are messy, your brain may well ignore or forget anything that contradicts that opinion. Your RAS will filter out all the times your children tidied up after themselves. It may well be they've been very happy to help, but they need you to ask them. Since you are focusing on the mess rather than your children's willingness to help, you end up making this opinion a self-fulfilling prophecy because you assume your children will always be messy and don't take steps to change it.

What you believe becomes your reality, regardless of whether it's actually true or not. The science of your RAS says so!

There is a little meditation you can do to help train your RAS to work on your behalf. First, think about a situation you'd like to influence. Maybe you'd like your children to help out more around the house. When you wake up in the morning, take 5 minutes to close your eyes, focus on your breath to ground and centre yourself, then create a mental film of what an ideal situation will be when you ask your children to help out. Try to make it as vivid as possible. How do the conversations go? What can you see? What are you all doing? Avoid letting any negative thoughts come in like, *That will never happen!* Just let your dream scenario play out.

Do this again last thing before you go to sleep at night and keep doing this on a daily basis. When you ask your children to help out, pay attention to what they do, rather than what they don't do. Actively encourage this behaviour and over time, you'll find reality shifts to get closer to your dream vision. It won't happen overnight, and things will never be as perfect as you want them to be, but it's amazing the difference it can make when you reprogram your brain to support what you want. This kind of exercise will enable you to be more patient when your children try to negotiate their way out of doing the chores and make you more tolerant when their efforts aren't quite up to your standards.

Meditation keeps your focus on a specific subject, which helps teach your brain how to refocus your attention. Some believe meditation can also activate your pineal gland, which handles information about the light-dark cycle in your environment so your brain can produce the right amount of melatonin, changing your perception and awareness.

Another meditation exercise you can do to reprogram your RAS is to go outside and look up at the sky. If that's not possible, you can lie on your bed and imagine you're outside. Start low and work your way up, looking at the trees, then the clouds, then the blue skies, then the sun and moon, then beyond that to space, the planets, stars, galaxies, going further and further until you reach the edge of the universe. This expands your awareness, where you realise you are very small in the grand scheme of things and whatever problems you're facing now will not be here tomorrow.

It is important that your core beliefs are only true for you, no matter how obvious you think they are, or how much you feel no other opinion is possible or can make sense given the evidence. It is more than possible for two people to look at the same piece of information and come to completely opposing opinions, both of which are equally valid.

So, when you observe an opinion coming into your mind, a statement that claims to be reality, start questioning whether it's really true. Is your partner truly negative or is it only you who sees this? Is your child really naughty or do you expect them to be, so they live up to your expectations?

Start setting an intention to be more open-minded towards the people around you. This will have positive benefits in all your relationships and not just those within your family. Increasing your emotional awareness and deciding that you want to be more accepting of your family and friends, your RAS will start working to filter out any information that doesn't fit into this new intention. Deciding your family love you and want the best for everyone in the home will help you see this more, making it easier for you to stay calm when things get tough.

action steps

- Go through this chapter and use the suggestions to put together a personalised stress management plan.
- Take some time to examine the beliefs and opinions you've been holding about your family. You might like to journal this to dig deep into the preconceived notions you have about everyone.
- Use the exercises in this chapter to start reprogramming your RAS to support a more positive outlook.
- Start meditating, even if it's only for a couple of minutes every day.
- When you're in a stressful situation, remember to breathe!

CHAPTER FIVE

*your child's emotional lighthouse –
where did that come from?*

Is 'ugh' an emotion? Because I feel it all the time – Unknown

A close friend of mine, Amelia, was pregnant with her second child. She was very excited about introducing her 4-year-old daughter, Charlie, to the new baby and thought she'd done a good job preparing her for meeting her sibling. She told her stories, showed her pictures from the scan and talked about all the fun things they could do once her baby brother arrived.

Amelia was scheduled to be induced, so Charlie went to stay with her grandmother while my friend was in hospital. It was a difficult birth and Amelia didn't want to upset Charlie by seeing her in a hospital bed, so the little girl didn't meet her brother until her mum was home and her grandmother brought her back.

Amelia told me she'd never forget the moment Charlie came into her bedroom where Amelia was nursing the baby.

'Are you excited to meet your brother, Xander?' she asked.

Charlie came over and looked the baby up and down. She shook her head.

'No,' she said. 'You need to send him back. He's not my brother.'

Amelia tried to explain that Xander was her brother and she couldn't send him anywhere, but Charlie was absolutely adamant that the baby had to go. She wanted a different brother, a better one. Charlie got so upset, she ended up on the floor kicking and screaming until her grandmother had to take her out of the room to calm down.

Fortunately, Charlie got used to the idea that her brother was here to stay and now the two of them are best friends, but it was touch and go for a while.

One of my clients has a 9-year-old son called Josh. She was going away with her husband on a much-needed weekend break. The pair of them worked long hours and rarely had any time to themselves, so they were both looking forward to having some time out.

Josh was going to stay with his aunt, who he didn't know very well, but my client assured him he'd have an amazing time. She had a pool and a horse, so he'd spend his days chilling out or going for long rides.

'You won't want to come home,' she told him.

Josh was really looking forward to going and, when his parents dropped him off, he was more than happy to wave goodbye to them.

My client had a wonderful few days with her husband and when they went to pick up Josh, they were looking forward to hearing all about how much fun he'd had with his aunt. Instead, as soon as he heard them at the door, he came running up to them.

'Thank goodness you're home!' he cried. 'If you'd stayed away any longer, I was going to run away. That woman is the worst person I've ever met in my life! She's mean, she's miserable and I don't want to ever see her again!'

Unfortunately for my client, his aunt was right behind Josh and heard everything he said.

Another client of mine was struggling to deal with her 15-year-old daughter Tonya.

'Every day's a struggle, Deborah,' she told me. 'It's not like I keep her locked up in her room or take her phone away. But if I ask her where she's going or who she's going to be with, all I get is eye rolls and big sighs.

'If I want to know what time she's leaving or when she's going to be back, she flips out on me like I'm the Spanish Inquisition. All I want to know is where she is so I can come get her if there's a problem, but she acts like I'm trying to control her. The other day, I went out to my car and saw she'd used chalk to write "Number One Bitch" next to my car, and all because I asked her to pick up her laundry before she went out.'

Our kids really know how to push our buttons. Half the problem is they've known us all their lives, so when you combine that with inheriting their personality traits from you, it can be tough to keep your cool. There are times when you just want to call your parents and apologise for everything you must have put them through.

There are 3 main areas that affect your child's behaviour:

1. **Genetics.** There's been a wealth of research into the idea of nature vs nurture and the evidence is overwhelming that children are born with certain traits that will make them easier or harder to parent. Many mental health conditions also have a genetic component. For example, if you have ADHD, your child has a 35% chance of also having the disorder. Likewise, if a child has ADHD, there is a 50% chance of at least one of their parents having it.[13]
2. **The way your child is disciplined.** When faced with a

child pushing the boundaries, it can be difficult to keep your cool and use the most appropriate form of discipline. It is also easy to accidentally ignore good behaviour and reward negative behaviour, making a situation worse, not better.

3. **Stressful situations.** Although we like to say that children are resilient, the reality is they are vulnerable to stressful situations. Moving home, changing schools, marital problems, financial difficulties and lack of friends can all increase the stress in the home. Even if a child isn't directly responsible for paying the bills, they can be impacted by your stress over a financial situation, which can be reflected in their behaviour.

Regardless of circumstance, most children will act out if they're frustrated or their needs aren't being met. If your child is misbehaving, don't try to stop them. Instead, **HALT!**

Take a moment to ask yourself whether your child is:

- **Hungry**
- **Angry**
- **Lonely or bored**
- **Tired**

Social psychologist Rudolf Dreikurs identified four main goals that drive misbehaviour:[14]

- **Attention**
- **Power**
- **Revenge**
- **Display of inadequacy**

So if you want to identify which goal is driving a misbehaviour, a good place to start is to examine how it makes you feel and how you would usually respond to it. Knowing which goal is at play will help you determine the best way of dealing with the situation.

be your child's emotional coach

Emotional coaching teaches your children emotional intelligence, including self-awareness, self-management, relationship management and social awareness. In my work, I've noticed that many parents overlook the importance of two of the biggest life lessons their children need to learn – how to regulate their feelings and how to understand how others feel.

Children learn their emotional intelligence from you. Not from television, social media, books or friends, but you. If you're not actively being your child's parental coach, you are missing out on a major opportunity to give your child the support they need. It's your role to support your child to recognise their feelings and be able to express them in age-appropriate ways.

Children who receive emotional coaching from their primary caregivers learn how to self-regulate their emotions and are better equipped to handle their emotional states.[15] This will serve them well when they transition to adulthood.

Emotional health is the number one factor that determines someone's quality of life, even more so than academic or career achievements. An unhealthy emotional state can cause children to lose their focus or motivation, negatively impacting on their ability to learn new things. Thus, someone's IQ (Intelligence Quotient) is directly linked to their EQ (Emotional Intelligence). Children who are able to manage their emotions, and as a consequence their behaviour, tend to be more self-disciplined, cooperative and confident.

The good thing is that it doesn't matter how old your child is – you can always start emotionally coaching them. You just need to adapt your approach according to their age and stage to give them the best support.

0 to 18 months

This age is all about building trust with your child. The

connections you form during this crucial early stage will shape the foundation of your relationship for the rest of your lives.

It is impossible to spoil a baby. Do not worry that in giving them what they need, you are somehow harming them. Your baby relies on you for absolutely everything and they need to know you will always be there for them if they have a problem. Whether your baby is crying out for food, comfort, warmth or a nappy change, when you promptly solve their problem, you build trust. Each cry has a distinct sound to tell you the problem, so, as you get to know your child's language, you'll become better at responding to your baby's needs.[16]

Studies have shown that babies' stress hormones increase when they hear angry voices, even if they're asleep.[17] This is why it's important to keep your voice calm, cuddle your baby and maintain eye contact to help them stay relaxed and learn that the world is a safe place. This will help teach your child self-regulation from a very early age, lowering the release of stress hormones, such as cortisol and adrenaline. It also means you're emotionally coaching your child – see how easy it can be?

18 months to 3 years

This can be the time when it feels like "no" is the only word in your vocabulary. Most parents dread the so-called "Terrible Twos". The problem is that now your child is walking and talking, it's easy to think they have greater control over their emotions and impulses than they actually do. Imagine being a little person with very little experience of the world. All you want to do is learn more about everything around you, but every time you try to stick toast in the DVD player or draw pretty pictures on the walls, you get yelled at and you have no idea why.

Toddlers are tiny balls of strong emotions and urges who don't yet have the mental capacity to control their impulses. They haven't got the ability to be rational and even if your toddler is highly talkative, they can't express their feelings because they don't even understand what a feeling is.

When they get upset, cortisol and adrenaline builds up in their little bodies to a point where it becomes overwhelming, and this is released through tantrums. The problem here is when they were a baby and cried, you gave them kisses and cuddles and fixed their problems. Now when they cry, you may get frustrated with them. It's a big shift in the behaviour of a previously nurturing parent, which confuses the toddler even more. When you look at it like this, is it any wonder the twos are so terrible for all of us?

Your toddler isn't having tantrums to annoy you. They can't control them. And if you inappropriately discipline a tantrum, you're more likely to experience actively defiant behaviour when they're older. Keep your voice calm, redirect your child when they misbehave and let the little things slide.

3 years to 7 years

There's a reason why the Jesuits say, 'Give me a child until he's 7 and I'll show you the man'. Those first 7 years are the most crucial for brain development. I personally believe these years set the foundation for how your child will emotionally experience the world in the future.

By giving your child a solid foundation through emotional coaching, they learn how to self-soothe and regulate their emotions in a healthy way. During this period, your child develops empathy and has more self-control. How they behave towards other children, and how much they want to help you, reflects the nature of the relationship they have with you.

At this stage, your child can name their feelings and express their emotions in a calm manner. By the age of 6, they can self-reflect and know what they can expect from their caregivers, both good and bad.

Strong relationships during this stage are the foundation of your child's resilience. Giving them a positive start in life will help them to cope better with any setbacks and deal with negative experiences in a healthy manner, setting them up to deal with any challenges that may come their way. You don't need me to tell you what an important skill this is to have as an adult.

During this phase, make sure you really listen to your child when they talk to you. Encourage their communication skills and make time to discuss their experiences.

7 years to 12 years

During this pre-teen or 'tween' stage, your child's world is expanding all the time. They're building new relationships, working their way through the school system, developing an understanding of culture and coming up with their own opinions about the world. They are developing a sense of self and what happens when they interact with others. They learn from their experiences to build strong relationships and have the ability to manage and express their emotions.

Despite these enhanced skills, there's still a lot of confusion for your child. They're in that in between stage of no longer being a little child, but they're not yet a teenager. Their bodies are changing on a daily basis, bringing a whole other set of problems. They crave more independence yet are still reliant on you for support, so it's common to have arguments over silly little things.

Continue building on the foundation you laid down in the early years. Maintain open communication, listen to them and stay connected. Show a genuine interest in the things they love and make time to give them your undivided attention. If your child says they need you and you really can't stop what you're doing, make sure you take time out for their problem or news as soon as you can.

Let your child know they will always be a high priority for you and you will keep your promises to them.

12 years to 18 years

Often the thing that sustains us through those sleepless nights and nappy-filled days is the thought that it will get easier when your child gets older. But then the teen years hit like a wrecking ball.

You may see your child's behaviour regress as hormones really take over their emotional reactions. Teenagers feel like they want to be adults but they're not quite ready, so this is the time when they start to rebel against the family rules. Sometimes, all you can do is stand back and watch your baby become an adult.

Stability is a good antidote to teenage angst, so if you haven't already, introduce family traditions, like pizza-making night or Sunday brunch, to build a strong sense of community and belonging. While your teen might not tell you these things matter to them, they really do.

Don't be afraid to talk about your feelings with your child. Be prepared to have some difficult conversations and plan for them. Respect your teen's need for privacy but let them know you're there when they need you. Keep your expectations realistic and don't take it personally when your teen acts out. You're their safe space, the one person they can trust to be there for them no matter what, so their outbursts are never personal.

Teenagers want their independence, so give them responsibilities and give them a say in family decisions. Ask for their opinions and take them on board – they may have better ideas than you on how to run the household!

If you are concerned about your relationship with your child, don't give up hope. Famous child psychologist Dr Dan Siegel[18] states that whatever the age or stage of your child, you can develop secure attachment with them by using the four Ss:

- **Seen.** This goes beyond physically looking at your child. It means perceiving them deeply and empathetically, tuning into the mind behind their behaviour. Dr Siegal calls this "mindsight".
- **Safe.** Build a safe environment for your child by avoiding actions or responses that frighten or hurt them.

- **Soothed.** Help your child deal with difficult emotions and situations with empathy, patience and understanding.
- **Secure.** Help your child develop an internalised sense of wellbeing or higher self-esteem.

Empathetic listening is an important part of this process. This involves being a caring, mindful listener so your child can gain clarity around their problems and emotions. When you give your child a safe space to problem solve and resolve conflict, you build respect, trust and mutual understanding with them that, in turn, encourages further sharing of feelings and information. It also reduces stress, strengthens relationships and relieves any tension or frustration.

Empathetic listening can take time to master because most people prefer to talk than listen. Even when someone else is talking, you're more focused on what you want to say next than hearing what it is they're actually saying.

Empathetic listening can be difficult because often it's needed the most when your child is in pain, angry or upset, which is when you're likely to be highly emotional as well. Commit to the process and don't be too hard on yourself when you slip up – it takes practice and dedication and there's always another opportunity to be an active, empathetic listener.

These are the steps to becoming an empathetic listener:
- Give your child your undivided attention when they talk and really listen to what they're telling you.
- Do not interrupt, even if you think your point is critical.
- Ask open-ended questions to get your child to elaborate on their feelings.
- Do not come to premature conclusions.
- Do not offer any solutions while your child is talking.
- Reflect back with your child what you heard them say to check you have truly understood what they've been trying to tell you.

- Allow your child to lead the conversation and choice of topic.

The great thing about empathetic listening is that once you start practising it, it benefits all your relationships, not just how you get on with your child. Empathy is not about feeling bad on behalf of your child. It's all about being willing to put yourself in their situation and understanding how they feel, even if this is not how you would feel, so they can be heard in a non-judgmental way.

action steps

- When your child misbehaves, pause so you can react with consideration instead of out of instinct. Ask yourself what the actual root cause of their behaviour might be. What need isn't being met? What is frustrating them?
- Identify the emotional stage of your child's development and use that to guide the way you interact with them.
- Start practising Dr Siegel's four Ss.
- Start being an empathetic listener. Use this in all your day-to-day interactions. Be an empathetic listener with your child, your colleagues, your friends, your families and strangers. The more you practise, the better you will be and the better your relationship with everyone around you.

CHAPTER SIX

building connection - where have my babies gone?

The only relationship I have is with my Wi-Fi. We have a connection
– Unknown

My friend, Britta, has a 15-year-old daughter called Hayley. Hayley was going through a rebellious phase, pushing the boundaries and really getting on Britta's last nerve. After a particularly nasty argument over grades, Britta grounded Hayley for 2 weeks. The only places Hayley was allowed to go to were school, the library and home.

Needless to say, Hayley wasn't very impressed by this, so she spent most of her time locked in her bedroom, refusing to talk to Britta beyond grunting in her general direction.

In the early hours of the morning one day, Britta woke up and needed to go to the bathroom. After doing her business, she came out, still half-asleep, to be confronted by the sight of Hayley creeping up the stairs. She was dressed as if she'd been to a party and reeked of cigarettes and alcohol. Britta didn't smoke nor keep any drinks in the house.

'Where do you think you've been?' Britta braced herself for a screaming argument.

Without skipping a beat, Hayley said, 'Late night study group at the library.'

'At 4 a.m. in the morning? Kiddo, you're going to have to do better than that, especially looking like *that*.'

'Okay.' Hayley sighed with a dramatic air. 'I didn't want to tell you, but Lily's parents are getting divorced. She came over and needed to talk so we went for a walk together.'

Hayley was so convincing that Britta gave her the benefit of the doubt.

'Alright. It's lovely that you care about your friend so much, but remember you're grounded, you're only 15 and it's the middle of the night. Next time talk to me and we can maybe arrange a sleepover, given the circumstances.'

'Sure, Mum.' Hayley kissed her mum on the cheek and went off to bed.

When I saw Britta and Hayley not long after, Britta gushed about what a caring child Hayley was and how much she felt really connected to her.

'There aren't many 15-year-olds who'll give their mum a kiss on the cheek,' she said.

I didn't have the heart to tell her that Hayley had told me the *real* story. Her friend had called to tell her there was a party happening at a boy's house; a boy Hayley had a huge crush on. His dad was away for the weekend and Hayley's friend thought this could be her opportunity for the two of them to get together.

'Best. Night. Ever!' Hayley said. 'I should never have been grounded in the first place. I've been working so hard on my schoolwork. I know I'm only getting Cs, but I *earn* those Cs. I'm just not the perfect A student Mum wants me to be and I never will be. I deserved that party, so I went and had a good time. If

Mum wasn't so hard on me, I'd have told her where I was going, but she'd never understand.'

I didn't want to burst Britta's bubble. She really felt the two of them had made a connection when, in fact, Hayley was lying to her because she didn't feel she could tell her mum the truth. If she was a client, I would have given her a few little tools she could use to improve her relationship with her daughter, but as a friend, I have to put my parenting coach hat to one side and just listen.

Marie, however, was a client of mine. She came to me for help because she felt like her son, Danny, was pulling away from her and she didn't like it.

'I just want my baby back,' she told me during a consultation. 'We used to be so close. Danny used to love it when we held hands. We'd skip along, singing songs and neither of us cared what anyone thought. Now he's 8 and he says he's too old for all that "stupid stuff". It's not stupid – it's our thing.

'The other day we were at the supermarket and I started singing the song we made up about baked beans and he ran into the next aisle so he wouldn't be seen with me. When I went after him, I tried to take his hand, but he put them in his pockets and refused to take them out. He said I was embarrassing. Embarrassing? Me? He was the one being embarrassing the way he was behaving.'

Another client of mine, Sophie, was upset about her daughter, Maeve, starting day-care. It wasn't that her little girl was going to be with someone else all day after spending the first few years at home with her mum; no, Sophie was upset because Maeve was loving it.

'When I took her there for the first time, Maeve walked in without a backwards glance,' Sophie told me. 'The staff commented on how confident she seemed, but I know my daughter. I was expecting her to get upset any minute as soon as she realised I wasn't going to be staying with her.

'I went to sit with the other mums whose children were starting that day. We were all anxious, biting our nails, stressing about how our babies were doing. You could hear children crying for their mums and I hated thinking about Maeve missing me like that.

'One of the staff came out and motioned to me to come talk to her. I hurried over, expecting to be asked to settle Maeve down. Instead, she told me I could go home because Maeve was playing happily in the sandpit. She'd chosen what she wanted for lunch and had already made a few friends. She reassured me Maeve was doing fine and wouldn't need me to wait for her.

'Well, Maeve might have been fine, but *I* wasn't. Those other mums all had to stay because their babies needed them. Mine couldn't care less if I was there or not. It was so embarrassing. I felt like a total failure. I'm such a terrible mother.'

Of course, I made sure she knew she wasn't a failure. The total opposite in fact. It was *because* of their strong connection that Maeve was settling so well. She'd been brought up in a safe, secure, loving environment and knew all was right in her world. If her mum had chosen that day care, it was because it was the absolute best place for Maeve to be. Sophie was an amazing mum and I was glad I was able to support her to see that.

So what is connection anyway?

It's all about spending quality time with your children. Connection comes from being emotionally and physically present for your child. You can be home 24/7 with them, but if you're ignoring them all that time because housework or social media is more important, or working from home and being too focused on deadlines to pay any attention to them, you won't have much of a connection with them.

Studies consistently show the best way to stop your teen from being negatively influenced by culture and peer pressure is for them to have a close relationship with their parents.[19] If a child doesn't have a strong relationship with their parents, born out of quality time together, they tend to have low self-esteem because they don't feel they're worth love. What's more, if you have a close bond with your child, you'll see less misbehaviour because your child will know they can always turn to you.

If your child feels connected to you, they don't feel alone, which is very important for all of us. Humans are herd animals. We need people around us for our self-worth, happiness and wellbeing, especially those people who are important to us – like our family. Feelings of loneliness are incredibly painful, especially for children because they're so dependent on us in those crucial early years.

Furthermore, that connection helps build confidence in your children, like Sophie's daughter, Maeve. It allows them to develop positive relationships with people outside the family, supporting them to create healthy relationships with their peers and other caregivers. However, for many parents, building a connection with their children can be challenging for a number of reasons:

- **You weren't connected with your own parents.** We look to our parents for lessons on how to bring up our own children, so if you had parents who weren't good at connecting with you for whatever reason, you may find it hard to connect with your own child. Difficult doesn't mean impossible, but it *does* mean you have to make a concerted effort to break the cycle.
- **You may be caught up in your own emotional state.** You may be too caught up in your own head, obsessing about your problems or worrying about the future. While it's understandable for you to be fretting about difficult situations in your life, if you're not living in the present moment, it's impossible for you to connect with your children.
- **You may be overcommitted.** If your day is filled with chores or work or you've over-filled your day with

stimulating activities for the children, you may struggle to connect. Sometimes we can get so caught up in the mistaken belief that the best thing we can do for our children is give them plenty of exciting experiences and lots of educational activities, but when that's what you spend all your time and energy on, you will be too tired to make any meaningful connection – that's assuming you've got any time available at all.

- **You may be going through life on autopilot.** When you feel so overwhelmed it's all you can do to get through the day, you're not really present at all. You don't feel any connection with yourself, let alone your children.

If you look back over your own childhood, you'll notice the best childhood memories all involve connection. Those times you think about most fondly are the ones when you felt most loved.

Fortunately, if you feel disconnected with your children, it's never too late to change that. It might take a lot of effort on your part, depending on how old your children are, but if you are persistent and consistent, you'll get there in the end.

There are a few ways you can start building a connection right now. For example, start living in the present moment by practising mindfulness. Mindfulness simply means being aware of what's happening in the present rather than obsessing over the past or worrying about the future. One simple way of doing this is to take a few moments to focus on your breath. Simply watch it flowing in and out without trying to control or change it in any way.

Another way is to pause and tune in to each of your 5 senses to check in with yourself in that moment. What can you see? Hear? Smell? Taste? Touch? The more mindful you are, the more you ground yourself, which will elevate your emotional state and change your thought patterns, making you more capable of being present for others.[20]

Reducing screen time is another way to build connection. There is an overwhelming amount of evidence of the negative impact of too much screen time[21] and there's no doubt that letting technology babysit your children can result in major disconnect. Limit your children's screen time – but also consider cutting back on your own. Be aware of how much family time is devoted to devices and look at other ways of entertaining everyone.

Schedule a specific time in your diary to connect with your children. It might seem forced, but if you're not used to building connection, the best way to ensure it happens is to actively set aside time for it. It doesn't have to be long. Just taking 15 minutes after dinner for a conversation can make a big difference.

We looked at empathetic listening earlier in the book, but I want to take a moment to remind you of this important skill. Listening without judgement is a great way to encourage your child to open up and make them feel safe and confident to talk to you about how they're feeling.

connection through the ages and stages

As the stories at the start of this chapter shows, as your child grows, they go through different stages of development, which means their need for connection will change, as will the way in which they experience it.

0 to 18 months

This period is all about establishing trust with your child. When your baby knows you will meet their basic needs – food, physical contact, clothing, etc. – their brain develops the capacity to effectively regulate stress and growth hormones. It is during this period that your child's nervous system and brain are hard wired for the rest of their life.

Connect with your child by: reacting to your baby's giggles and cries. Exaggerate your facial expressions and gestures. Give them plenty of cuddles. Spend time singing to them, reading stories or playing games like peekaboo or tickling their tummy. There is no way to spoil a baby, so give them as much love and attention as you can.

18 months to 3 years

Toddlers are starting to develop a distinct sense of self, viewing themselves as separate from their primary caregivers. They want more independence over things like feeding and dressing themselves without feeling like you're rejecting them by giving them too much independence. They'll assert themselves by using their favourite word "No"! This is the time for them to learn boundaries and limitations, such as needing to stay away from dangerous situations like hot stoves and stairs.

Connect with your child by: getting active. Take your toddler for walks and talk to them about what you encounter. Let them have lots of sensory play and if they seem bored, redirect their attention.

3 years to 7 years

During this period, your child is learning about what is real and what is imagined. This is a very imaginative, creative time for your child. Wanting to learn about pregnancy and birth is very common at this stage.

Connect with your child by: reading to them and playing word games like I Spy. Listen to music and play age-appropriate cards or board games. There will be lots of questions during this stage, so be prepared to answer them or rediscover the wonder of Google!

7 years to 12 years

During the tween years, children develop the values that will guide their decision-making and interests. You'll start to get a glimpse of the person your child will grow up to be. Friendships with peers become very important, although there may also be a focus on competition and performance.

Connect with your child by: playing board games or going for bike rides. Take up a sport or hobby you can all enjoy together.

12 years to 18 years

These are the years when hormones rule! This can be a really challenging time of adjustment for both parent and child. Your teenager is establishing their identity in terms of how they relate to society, the opposite sex and their culture. They're starting to think about the future and what they may like to do. They'll crave independence, which can lead to clashes of opinion over what's appropriate and what's not.

Connect with your child by: asking how your child's day was and listening empathetically to the answer. Find out about their interests and whether you can join in. Continue to make one on one time for your child – it's even more important now. You might even like to set aside some time for day trips to create positive memories your child will treasure forever.

Connection should be a daily habit. It's something that strengthens over time, so make it a habit every day for your children. You could make evenings family time when you switch off the television, put the phones away and enjoy dinner together. If that's all you do, it's a huge step towards building close family bonds. You could extend this to playing games or hanging out together after the meal is over.

Set aside at least 10-20 minutes for each child so you can talk. This is about bonding through getting to know each other, so try not to fill the time with distractions like games or activities.

Give plenty of hugs. Children need physical affection from their loved ones – as I love to say, 'Fifteen hugs a day keeps the meltdowns at bay!'

Be present with your child and practise empathetic listening. Try to focus on the present moment when you're with your children. Don't let yourself get distracted by thoughts, text messages or worries.

Another meaningful way to build connection with your family is to hold regular family meetings. These are a good way to deal with any conflict, encourage open communication, plan what you're going to do together, agree on any family rules and problem solve together. This teaches your children how to express their opinions respectfully, make decisions cooperatively and learn problem solving skills. These meetings give everyone the chance to discuss what's important to them, improve communication and nurture positive relationships.

If family meetings are a new concept for your family, they can seem quite daunting to your children because they might view them as just another way for parents to lay down rules and restrictions. On the flip side, parents might have concerns that a meeting will result in their children questioning their authority. This can mean that both sides avoid holding meetings because of a fear of conflict, the very opposite of what the meetings are supposed to achieve! In fact, when a family meeting is held properly, they're a great way for everyone to be seen, heard and understood.

I recommend you start family meetings when your children are at least 4. Everyone should be encouraged to contribute, and you should have a structure to your meeting, which shouldn't last more than an hour, or less if your children are young. It can be nice to have a fun activity planned at the end of the meeting, like a board game.

Put together an agenda for the week's meeting. You might like to have a bulletin board or notebook available where everyone can write down the things they'd like to discuss or activities they want to plan.

A structure that works well might look like this:

Open the meeting with a short little ritual that reflects your family personality and values. This could be a poem, prayer, song, candle-lighting – whatever makes sense to you.

Express your gratitude for every family member, giving them a compliment and acknowledging their positive achievements in the week. This could be a good grade or simply commenting on good behaviour.

Have a discussion for about 15-20 minutes on a topic you are all interested in. This could be current affairs, music, religion, or anything that interests you all. Make sure everyone is supported to share their opinions.

Review the week by discussing what went well for you all, what went wrong and what you want to work on in the week to come. This is all about working as a unit rather than looking at individual issues.

Deal with any problems. Look at your agenda or the notes people have made during the week to tackle any problems. Try to stick to one issue, but if there's more than one that needs your attention, either make it a priority for the following week or setting aside extra time on another day to deal with it. Give each family member a time limit to give their perspective on the problem and listen without judgement. Ask everyone to suggest solutions and discuss them to come to an agreement. If you can't come to a consensus, leave the problem for now and come back to it later. It can be difficult to find a solution if everyone's feeling emotional, so sometimes the best thing to do is give everyone some time.

Plan the week ahead. Think about what you might like to do in the coming week. This could be fun things like day trips or going to the movies, but it can also include household chores and assigning them to individuals. Synchronise your calendars with agreed goals and tasks.

End the meeting with something fun. This could be playing a game, watching a movie, making a meal together or enjoying a takeaway. Let everyone take a turn in choosing what you're going to do that week for fun.

action steps

- It's never too late to build connection with your family. You can consciously start building it on a daily basis. Set aside time every day for one-on-one time with each of your children.
- Start practicing mindfulness to be in the present moment.
- Reduce screen time.
- Remember to practise empathetic listening.
- Connect with your child according to their age and stage.
- Start holding regular family meetings. Have an agenda agreed in advance and plan something fun for when you've finished.

CHAPTER SEVEN

*mastering communication -
am i speaking a foreign language?*

I guess I'm quite used to not being understood than being understood
– Bjork

I took Grace to the playground one day. Seeing that nobody was on her favourite climbing frame, she started running towards it. I could see she was about to hit her head on it, so I yelled at her, 'Grace! Duck!' She looked at me, puzzled.

'Duck? Where? Quack!'

Not seeing a duck anywhere, she turned back to the climbing frame... and promptly hit her head.

I'm really enjoying the toddler stage, but there are times when I'll be glad when Grace has a stronger command of the language. She struggles to pronounce the "tr" sound at the beginning of words, which comes out as more of an "f" sound. I'll leave to your imagination what she yells at the top of her voice whenever she spots a truck!

It's not just young children who can make mistakes with their communication though. Remember my friend Britta? When Hayley was younger, around eight, one of Britta's old school friends came to visit. They hadn't seen each other since before Hayley was born, so Britta and her friend had a lovely afternoon catching up on all the gossip of the previous years.

When it was time for her friend to go, Britta called Hayley to come say goodbye.

'Goodbye and good riddance.' Hayley smiled.

Britta was shocked until she found out that Hayley thought that "good riddance" meant it was good to see you. Apparently, she'd been saying it to her friends for ages!

One of my clients had sent her 10-year-old son to the local Catholic school. They weren't a particularly religious family, but the school had a strong academic reputation and she figured the nuns would be able to keep him out of mischief. Unfortunately, it wasn't really working. She'd been called into the school a few times to talk about Harry's behaviour. The latest escapade had involved an incident in confession. They had been discussing the ten commandments in class beforehand, but the nun wouldn't go into detail about what adultery involved, simply that it was an adult matter.

Harry decided it would be fun to tell the priest that he'd been committing adultery on a regular basis. The priest hadn't been able to stop himself from yelling, 'Are you serious?' which could be heard throughout the church.

Although the priest wasn't allowed to tell anyone what Harry had said, Harry happily told everyone the sin that had got the priest so upset.

When asked why he'd done it, Harry innocently replied, 'I thought adultery meant pretending to be an adult.' My client still isn't sure whether this is true or not.

If you think it's bad trying to communicate with younger children, I'm afraid to tell you, it doesn't really get any better as they get older. Are you up to date with all the latest slang and acronyms? One of my clients told me about the time her teen texted to tell her she'd got an A in her history test. My client wrote back, 'WTF!!!' She thought it stood for, 'Well that's fantastic...'

Another client was getting frustrated with their teenage son ignoring all her texts. She'd been sending them asking him to do various household chores or reminding him of things they had planned and would get nothing back, not even a thumbs up emoji. At last, she sent him a message reading, 'Your dad and I have decided you need more responsibility so we're going to get you a puppy. Make sure you walk it every day.'

Her son wrote back, 'Seriously? All those years of asking and you're finally letting me have a dog! You're the best!'

'No, we're not getting a dog. I was just checking your texts are still working.'

Needless to say, we worked on healthier ways of communicating without playing games. Let's be honest, even adults have problems with communicating effectively, so what hope do our kids have?

Children learn from their environment and pick up their communication skills predominantly through interacting with their family, at least in the early years. Unfortunately, if you're not aware of how you're communicating with your child, you may fall into one of many common parenting traps, which include:

- **Accidental rewards.** You reward your child for misbehaviour, for example, buying them a treat while out shopping to keep them quiet.
- **Paying attention to unwanted behaviours.** Children crave attention from their parents and caregivers. If you've not been making time for your child, then they'll decide that any attention is good attention and start acting out to get some kind of response from you.

- **Ignoring wanted behaviour.** Likewise, if you're not giving your child any attention when they're behaving in a way you want, you'll teach them the way to get noticed is to misbehave.

The worst types of parenting traps, however, are escalation traps. These can create a hostile environment and cause both parent and child to see their emotions spiral out of control. These escalating behaviours can be easy to spot since they generally follow a 4-step process: "Talk, Persuade, Argue, Hit Syndrome", a term used by child psychologist Thomas W Phelan.[22]

Let's look at what happens when your child starts escalating. Let's say they want something, but you're ignoring them. They start to turn up the volume, becoming more demanding and louder. They might yell, stamp their foot, or throw a tantrum. Right when they're at their worst, you finally relent and let them have whatever it was they asked for in the first place. Anything to stop the noise, right? And what have you taught your child? When they don't get what they want, the best thing to do is escalate.

Parents can do this too. Let's say you ask your child to set the table for dinner. They say they're too busy, so you get louder, possibly even threatening them. It's only when you've completely lost it that your child finally gets up and deals with the table. So, what have you realised? The only way to get your child to cooperate is to yell and get angry with them.

It's very easy to fall into the trap of giving your child lots of attention when they're misbehaving. It's only natural after all – emotions are running high, and you need to deal with the situation. The problem is if you don't deal with it appropriately, you're accidentally rewarding your child with lots of attention for their misbehaviour.

In contrast, when your child is behaving well, the reward they get tends to be boring, unexciting or delayed – assuming they get any reward at all.

It's not difficult to see this combination of responses is more likely to increase your child's misbehaviour because they're getting a reward for acting out, even if that reward is negative attention. If that's the only attention they're getting, they'll take it!

So you need to flip this on its head. Make your approach to discipline boring, dull and uneventful, while rewarding positive behaviours with excitement, encouragement, interest and positivity.

These rewards don't have to cost any money. For example, you can use describing praising, where you notice your child's positive behaviour and praise them while describing the exact behaviour you admired. For example, 'Thank you for loading the dishwasher. I really appreciate that I only had to ask you once.'

Physical affection is another good way – hugs, kisses, high fives, etc. all reward your child and cost nothing. If you do want to give tangible rewards, these can be small such as stickers, treat food, extra screen time or a toy. However, I advise against relying on these too heavily because children will start to expect a bribe every time you want them to do something.

The most powerful reward you can give is your time and attention. You could play a game or read a book or even go out somewhere like the park or swimming pool. Be unpredictable with your rewards, using different approaches all the time so your child receives positivity in a variety of ways without expecting anything. Reward positive behaviour as much as you can and ignore anything else.

Be consistent with your rewards. It might take a while for you to see the change in your child's behaviour you'd like but persevere – your hard work will pay off in time. Make sure you regularly reflect on the results of your rewards. You might need to tweak what you're doing to best suit the needs of your child.

Adjust your language. Instead of making treats conditional, such as, 'You can only have half an hour of screen time if you clean up your room,' use when/then sentences like, 'When you clean up your room, then you can have half an hour of screen time.'

Let's look a little closer at the impact of your body language when you deal with your child. Studies show that the tone of your voice and your body language make up as much as 93% of the information you communicate to others. This means just 7% of our communication come from our words.

Do you remember when someone told you they were fine, but their head and shoulders were drooping, they couldn't meet you in the eye and their tone was downbeat? Did you *really* think they were fine, or did you know that something was wrong? But if they say they're fine and they've got a huge grin on their face, their tone is upbeat and they're virtually dancing with excitement, you'd think something incredible had happened to them, wouldn't you?

Your emotions have a direct impact on the tone of your voice, which impacts on the direction of your conversation far more than words alone do. This is also why there can be so much miscommunication on the internet – remove the body language and tone from the equation and you're far more likely to be misinterpreted.

When you control the emotion and motivation you're expressing while you talk, you can influence and improve your communications.[23] You may not have been aware of how the tone of your voice has been impacting on the relationship you have with your child. If they run up to you all excited about a pretty stone they've found and you barely look at them while you grunt, 'That's nice,' they're going to rightly assume you don't care about something important to them.

Every time you talk, you have the chance to convey a message *and connect and develop relationships.* Children don't really listen to your words so much as the emotion behind them, whatever that may be. Your parenting voice can be calming, friendly and inspiring or it can be aggressive, loud and intimidating. When you know how to use your body language and tone to engage and guide your children, you'll see a dramatic improvement in your relationship.

You probably don't remember what it was like to be a toddler or tween. We all have funny stories about kid logic that makes absolutely no sense to us but is perfectly reasonable to your child, but to a child, adult logic can make no sense. What do you mean your child can't eat worms? They're delicious! When a child doesn't understand what you want from them or your motives for asking, this can trigger testing and manipulation.

The 3 main causes of frustration between parent and child are:
- When you ask your child to stop doing something they're enjoying
- When you ask your child to start doing something they don't want to
- Not giving them something they want.

When your child feels frustrated, they have two choices: go along with what you want and deal with their frustration. This is difficult for little ones but it gets easier as they mature and develop emotional intelligence. Or test and manipulate you to avoid discipline, leaving you feeling emotionally confused and side tracked.

Ask any parent of a toddler or older child and they'll tell you their child is a past master of manipulation. Some common tactics include:
- **Pestering.** 'Mum! Mum! Mum! Mum! Why can't I? Why? Why? Why? Why?' Constantly going on about something is designed to wear you down so you'll give in to their demands to get some peace.
- **Threatening.** They might tell you they won't love you or they won't do their chores if you don't give them what they want.
- **Temper outbursts.** Tantrums or yelling, 'I hate you!'

before stomping off to their room can occur if you try to use too many words with your child or your child knows you struggle to cope with their aggression. This is particularly common with toddlers who have little control over their emotions and rely on you to stay calm and help them weather the storm.
- **Being charming.** Telling you how wonderful you are or promising to be good is a guilt trip designed to make you feel bad for frustrating your child. They're trying to negotiate with you so you'll compromise and let them have what they want because they're being just so good.
- **Physical violence.** Hitting, biting, breaking things, etc. are all examples of this. They're common in younger children, but if this behaviour continues after your child reaches the age of 4 it is a cause for concern. I'd advise seeking professional help if this is the case for you.
- **Trying to guilt you.** Telling you what a terrible parent you are or how you always want your child to be miserable is often combined with sad expressions or even tears so you feel awful and give your child what they want.

Whatever tactic your child uses, they all have the same underlying message: 'You've made me feel uncomfortable, so I'm doing the same to you. I'll stop if you do.'

non-violent communication

I strongly recommend the book *Non-violent Communication* by Marshall B. Rosenburg[24] to anyone who wants to improve their communication skills. Practicing the core principles of non-violent communication (NVC) won't just improve your interactions with your children but with everyone around you.

If you're judging others, bullying, ruled by bias, blame, discriminate, speak without listening, criticise, name call, act defensively or angrily, etc. you are communicating violently. In comparison, NVC is a process developed by Rosenburg that focuses on 3 aspects of communication:

1. **Self-empathy.** A deep and compassionate awareness of your own inner experience.
13. **Empathy.** Understanding and sharing an emotion expressed by someone else.
14. **Honest self-expression.** Being able to authentically express your emotions in a way that may inspire compassion in others.

NVC brings together consciousness, language, communication and means of influence to combine them into an effective strategy. It has its roots in the concept that all people have the capacity of compassion and only turn to violence or harmful behaviour when they don't have better ways of meeting their needs. It has four components – observations, feelings, needs and requests – and uses honest expression and empathic receiving through these four components. It allows you to connect empathetically with others as well as yourself to enjoy more satisfying relationships.[25]

action steps

- Take time out to journal the behaviours you would like to see in your child in various situations.
- Once you have identified what you feel is optimal behaviour, make sure you pay attention when your child displays those behaviours and immediately respond to them with excitement, being genuinely and emotionally involved.
- Start rewarding these behaviours with descriptive praise, tangible rewards, physical affection or your time. Remember that your time is the most powerful reward there is, so try to give as much of it as you can.

- Be aware of your body language and tone when communicating with your child. Make your tone and body language as boring as possible when dealing with unwanted behaviours while being exciting and interested when your child is behaving well.
- Consider what your child's preferred testing and manipulation tactics are. Identify a few occasions recently when your child has used them. What was the result? What could you have done differently? What will you do differently moving forward?
- Study non-violent communication and start using it in all your interactions with your family. You may want to consider using it in other situations as well.
- If you feel your child is old enough and you have mastered the principles of NVC, start teaching it to your child. Teaching them how to communicate effectively is one of the greatest gifts you can give them.
- If you'd like reading suggestions that build on the principles outlined in this chapter, you can go to the resources page on my website at www.deborahbyrne.com

CHAPTER EIGHT

guidance and direction - please not another tantrum!

We never really grow up... We only learn how to act in public –
Bryan White

When my friend Amelia's youngest son, Xander, was 2, she told me about the time she was driving with her boys and a driver pulled out on them, almost sideswiping the car. Amelia reacted instinctively, yelling at him, 'You f**king *sshole! Why don't you watch where you're going?'

In the heat of the moment, shaken at almost being crashed into, she forgot to mind her language in front of the boys.

She was reminded why she didn't swear around the children when she was at the playground with the boys. Another child accidentally bumped into Xander and he yelled, 'You f**king *sshole! Why don't you watch where you're going?'

It was *really* hard for her to get him to stop calling anyone who annoyed him a f**king *sshole because he would look up at her with his big blue eyes and say, 'But Mummy. That's what *you* said.'

Another friend of mine, Karen, had 10-year-old twins, a boy

and girl called Ricky and Rachel. She'd always struggled to discipline her children – she's one of the sweetest people I know, but she was never able to assert herself when it came to her twins. She asked me for advice and I suggested she used break time, a discipline strategy similar to time out. We'll be going into it in more detail later in this chapter.

Karen did what I suggested and at first it seemed to be working. But then she noticed that whenever the children did something to push the boundaries, before Karen could even say anything, they'd ask if they could go into break time. It got to the point where the twins were deliberately misbehaving so they could be put into break time. Karen couldn't understand it, so she asked me to figure out what was going wrong.

I went over to her house for the afternoon, and it wasn't long before Ricky and Rachel got into a fight.

'That's it! Go to break time,' Karen said.

The twins grinned and raced off. Intrigued, I went after them and that's when I found out what was happening. They were being sent to the playroom filled with toys, books and a PlayStation! Break time was a major treat for them, not the time for reflection it was meant to be. No wonder the twins were choosing to act out.

Tonya is someone I've known since we were at school. She's an English teacher now, teaching unruly teens the difference between adjectives and verbs. She's always telling me funny stories about her students, but there was one in particular that really stood out to me.

There was one girl who didn't do her homework. When asked why she hadn't completed the assignment, her reply was that her mum had brought home a new puppy. She'd wanted to play with the puppy instead of doing the homework and her mum had said it was fine, so she didn't have time to write the essay. It seemed a little farfetched, so Tonya rang her mother to find out that yes, they had just got a puppy, yes, her daughter was too tired from playing with the puppy to do her homework and yes, she'd said it was fine for her to do her homework another day. To add insult to injury, the mum said she didn't see the point of studying English anyway – it wasn't like it was an important subject. I really felt for Tonya. It's so hard to discipline a group of unruly teens and it's even harder when you don't have the support of their parents.

Discipline is one of the trickiest issues for us to tackle as parents. This is why this chapter is going to be a long one, so buckle up!

First of all, I want to say I prefer to call discipline strategies "direction strategies" because all you're ever really doing is redirecting your child's misbehaviours. Many parents struggle to find the right balance between giving their children a degree of autonomy and being too strict. Personally, I feel we're there to guide our children and direct them to the best way to deal with any given situation. Discipline isn't a bad thing – it's how you implement it that makes all the difference.

To start, it's a good idea to establish household rules that everyone can agree to (when they're old enough). These rules are a good way to give your child a very clear idea of expectations of behaviour in any given situation, as well as what the consequences will be should they break any of the rules.

When coming up with your rules, it's better to keep them simple and have as few as possible. This makes it easy for your child to follow and easy for you to enforce. Be as specific as possible. Something like 'Be good' is meaningless to a child. What does that look like? Going to bed on time? Finishing all the food on your plate? Holding your hand when you're out? It's much better to be clear on the behaviour you'd like to see, for example, 'Follow Mum and Dad's instructions.'

Your rules need to be age appropriate – you can't expect a toddler to make their own bed perfectly! They should be realistic as well. A rule that states 'Always be good at home' is unrealistic.

Everyone has their good and bad days and sometimes your child needs to feel they can let go, even if it's not in a way you'd prefer.

It's also important that everyone in the house follows the rules, including you. Children learn from watching and will follow your behaviour more than they will your words, so be consistent and lead by example.

Keep rules positive, describing what you want your child to do, not what you don't want them to do. It's better to say, 'We all walk inside the house' than 'Don't run around the house.'

If you're facing repeat problem behaviours, rules are a great way of working with them.

If you're not sure where to get started with your family rules, here's a few ideas for you:

- Follow Mum and Dad's instructions.
- We all walk inside the house.
- We use our quiet voice inside the house.
- We sit at the table to eat our meals.
- Keep your hands and feet to yourself.
- Go to all the family meetings.
- Tell the truth.
- Tidy up after yourself.

The fewer rules the better. If you have a long list, it becomes complicated and confusing to remember, especially for little ones.

When you're putting together your rules, remember you want the whole family to follow them. It's fine to want your child to go to bed at a certain time, but you shouldn't make a family rule that states, 'Bedtime is at 7 p.m.' unless you want the whole family to go to bed at 7!

We've talked about family meetings in a previous chapter. A family meeting is the ideal time to discuss the rules you all want to implement. If you can involve your children in establishing the family rules, the more likely it is they'll understand and follow them.

Once you've talked through all the rules you'd like to establish

– and getting your children's input on what they think should be included – write them down and display them somewhere visible, such as on the fridge door or in the hall. You might even like to put up more than one copy if your home is large.

You are less likely to see difficult behaviour from your children if you act as their guide and mentor rather than being a strict authoritarian or doling out unfair punishments. You need to walk that very fine line between holding firm boundaries and allowing your child space. It's hard – trust me, I know! You're going to have good and bad days, so be kind to yourself when you're struggling. Every day gives you a chance to learn and do better next time. It's not always going to be sunshine and roses, so stay committed to the long-term process rather than fixating on a specific outcome in any given moment. As your child grows, you'll need to adjust how you guide your child.

0 to 13 months

Once your baby becomes mobile, it feels like a never-ending game of stopping them doing something that will hurt themselves. Babies want to experience the world with all their senses, which means they'll often put things in their mouth you really don't want them to. Since everything is so new to them, they haven't yet learned what's safe and what's not and they're desperate to experience their environment.

Fortunately, babies are easily distracted in that first year, so discipline for these little ones simply involves redirection and setting safe limits. Make sure you childproof your home as much as possible – you can use stairgates to keep your baby in a room, as well as stop them going up and down stairs.

Avoid using the word "no" unless it's an absolute emergency and they're about to seriously hurt themselves. Even then, it's better to use short descriptions, such as, 'Hot! The stove is hot!'

Babies simply don't have the ability to understand the concept of danger, so avoid yelling, punishments or dealing with them as if they are able to recognise, reflect or resolve. As with all direction strategies, remember to treat your baby in a way that is appropriate to their age and stage and have age-appropriate expectations of them.

13 to 36 months

This is when toddlers start breaking out and wanting independence from their caregivers. This age group is developing their sense of self and will start having their own opinions.

We joke that a toddler's favourite word is "no" but have you ever thought to ask why? It has been claimed that toddlers hear the word "no" an incredible 400 times a day.[26] We say no to toddlers all the time.

'No, you can't eat that worm.'

'No, you can't stick toast in the DVD player.'

'No, you can't give the dog a haircut.'

Why are we then surprised when our toddler says no to us?

Toddlers understand the word "no" as a way of asserting themselves and it's a healthy part of their development to express themselves by saying it. As long as they aren't putting themselves or anyone else in any danger, avoid punishing them for saying "no" – you want your child to grow up feeling confident in expressing themselves.

Toddlers are filled with strong wants and needs, which are greater than their willingness to cooperate with adults, so be prepared to practise lots of redirection and set empathetic limits. And much as it might be tough at times, remember that tantrums are a normal part of childhood development that need you to be patient and empathetic. Even if the sound of your toddler screeching gets on your last nerve.

3 to 5 years

At this age, your child is developing self-management. They're old enough to know the rules, but they'll still break them regularly, pushing your boundaries.

The problem is, they don't yet have the ability to regulate their behavioural impulses. Their brain is still going through a rapid rate of development, so they're filled with curiosity about their environment, making them easily distracted.

At this age, they're likely to be at kindergarten or school and that can fill their emotional backpack to overflowing. The only safe place your child can unload those emotions is at home with you. Yay! Don't you just love not seeing your child all day only to be faced with attitude and tantrums when they're back home?

Put yourself in their shoes. They're concentrating all day at school, which is absolutely exhausting. They need a safe place to express the emotions they couldn't let out anywhere else. However, the more disconnected a child is from their parents, the more likely they are to misbehave, so be sure to build your connection following the advice given earlier in this book. Give them special time and undivided attention so they feel safe in discussing their feelings to reconnect with you and regulate their emotions.

6 to 9 years old

Your child is now able to self-regulate their emotions. A child raised by calm, assertive parents, who have empathetic listening skills, will be better equipped to manage their emotional states and minimise tantrums. Their focus will be more directed towards learning new things than misbehaving. That doesn't mean you won't experience challenging times – there's still sibling rivalries to navigate, misbehaviours and pushing boundaries, but this is all a normal part of childhood development. The more you understand what's normal and what's not, the easier it becomes to deal with it.

Surviving these years involves plenty of hands-on interaction and a continuation of daily routines and structure. Consistently referring back to your household rules is a good way of reminding your child of what you expect. Their focus is more on learning new things and figuring out how to cope with social experiences.

Although your child is a lot more verbal now, try not to

overwhelm them with too much information. Practise undivided attention to maintain your connection. By now your child has the ability to reflect, realise and resolve, so it's a good time to start having more involved conversations about their experiences.

9 to 12 years old (or the tween years)

This group features resistance and regression. Not quite a teenager but no longer wanting to be a little child, they switch between craving independence and depending on their caregivers. This can be a difficult time for you too – you may feel like your child is pulling away from you and doesn't want your undivided attention anymore. However, no matter what their attitude, they still need time with you, so make sure you continue to actively listen, play games, hold family meetings and discuss their problems.

the teen years – yikes!

The family dynamic changes massively during the teen years. Your child is likely to want their privacy and prefer to spend time with their friends over you. However, they'll still need connection with you, so continue with your family meetings, sit down for meals together and arrange outings. Make your teen feel like they're part of a team and don't be afraid to ask for their advice.

During this period, your child's emotions and behaviours can be the most challenging yet, so set and maintain clear boundaries and use calm, assertive communication to resolve any conflicts. Yelling at your teen will only result in them yelling back at you. If an argument feels like it's going round in circles, try to defuse it and look to discuss the problem later when you've all calmed down.

breaktime

At the start of this chapter, I mentioned how I like to use breaktime as opposed to timeout. Some parents have an issue with the notion of timeout, but there is a lot of research to support the benefits of breaktime when it's used correctly – and not like Karen did![27]

Many parents think the only point of breaktime is to give your child a chance to think about what they did wrong. In fact, the main point of breaktime is to briefly remove attention from your child, avoiding accidentally rewarding misbehaviour and de-escalating the situation so you can get back to what you were doing as soon as possible.

Set aside a specific area to be used for breaktime. This should be somewhere free from distractions or anything your child might find entertaining. Decide how long you want your child to be calm for – this could be a minute per year of age or three minutes maximum and let your child know you'd like them to be calm for that entire time. If they misbehave, the timer starts again.

Be aware, if your child suffers from separation anxiety or has experienced trauma in the past, it is a good idea to conduct breaktime somewhere where you'll be visible to your child at all times. If you have any serious concerns about your child's behaviour, I always advise consulting a professional before you implement any of the strategies in this book.

When used properly, breaktime is an effective disciplinary approach that allows you to set reasonable limits on your child's behaviour by being gentle and supportive yet firm and instructive. You should only use it when other preventative strategies such as empathetic listening, planned ignoring or redirection are inappropriate for whatever reason. If there has been major misbehaviour, such as physical violence, you should go straight to breaktime without warning.

Before putting your child in breaktime, give them a clear start/stop instruction so they know what they're doing wrong and what you'd like them to do instead: 'I need you to stop playing with the cat and help me put away the toys.'

If they don't stop the unwanted behaviour, breaktime briefly separates them from a reinforcing environment so you can calm down conflict, reduce unwanted behaviours and teach your child self-regulation over their emotions. It takes them away from doing something fun, but it's important to forgive and forget once breaktime is finished. Don't expect your child to apologise once breaktime is done and don't lecture them. You might like to do something neutral like getting a glass of water together or reward the next positive behaviour from your child.

Breaktime should absolutely **not** be:
- A chance for your child to think about their behaviour and apologise for it
- Painful isolation from the family
- Something to blame your child for: 'You've been bad and now you've made me punish you. This is your own fault'
- Used without warning or the opportunity to improve behaviours
- Used inconsistently
- Used without explanation with a child who doesn't understand how breaktime works
- Used when you're angry or frustrated
- Used in addition to harsh punishments with consequences
- A way to shame your child
- The chance to debate with your child about their behaviour.

Before putting your child in breaktime, count to 3. This helps you to stay calm and also gives your child a warning that a consequence for their behaviour is coming. With older children, you can count to 3 before using an alternative to breaktime, such as losing a privilege.

Counting to 3 has a number of benefits. It lowers the risk of two of the most common discipline mistakes – talking too much and letting emotions run wild. Physically showing your fingers as you count pulls your child's attention to your body language, which makes it less aggressive. This also gives another consistent, predictable body language your child understands and means they need to change their behaviour. I've seen some of my clients redirect their child's behaviour without saying a word, simply holding up 1 or 2 fingers to warn them they will be in breaktime if they continue.

Counting to 1 and 2 gives your child a chance to change their behaviour. If they are doing something that is completely unacceptable, such as being physically aggressive, you can skip straight to 3.

Once you've mastered how to make breaktimes work for your kids,[28] it gives you an important, powerful tool to add to your redirection toolkit.

quiet time

Quiet time is similar to breaktime, but where you should have a designated area in your home for breaktime, quiet time is when you haven't got a specific area or can't get to your breaktime area. So, for example, if you're out with your child and they won't put their phone away when you've asked them to, follow the breaktime process but, rather than sending your child away, you say, 'It's quiet time now. Give me your phone and we'll just stand here for a few minutes.'

Quiet time works best if your child is already familiar with breaktime or is older in age. Once you've established breaktime with your child and it's working well, you might like to switch to quiet time. You would still count to 3, but instead of your child going to a separate area, you can ask them to sit quietly somewhere close like on a chair or sofa. You can use breaktime as a backup if your child isn't quiet during quiet time.

Here's some of the most common questions I get asked about breaktime:

'Should I explain why my child is going into breaktime?'

Breaktime works best when you've given a stop/start instruction and then counted to 3. Avoid getting drawn into a discussion with your child about the situation. It's a good idea to explain the breaktime process to your child before you start using it, so your child knows what will happen and also there may be times when they'll have to go to breaktime without this warning, skipping counts 1 and 2 and going straight to 3. Your child will very quickly learn to recognise '1... 2...' as a warning sign and know this is their chance to change what they're currently doing.

'Is it okay to reassure my child before or during breaktime?'

You should minimise interaction and emotion on the way to breaktime. It's best to stay calm and professional, not getting involved in a discussion or giving your child any physical attention. If you reassure your child with a hug, you're accidentally rewarding your child for their misbehaviour. Breaktime is intended to be boring.

'Should I use breaktime for all misbehaviour or can I ignore it sometimes?'

Save breaktime for behaviours that are non-negotiable. If your child is only minorly misbehaving, it's better to use planned ignoring, empathetic listening, redirection or anything else you find works without rewarding the misbehaviour. You know your child best, so use your intuition when it comes to choosing the right strategy.

> 'Sometimes I'm tired and don't feel like waiting for breaktime to be over or for my child to stop escalating. Can I cut it short sometimes?'

For breaktime to work, your child needs to stay in it until they're calm and quiet. They shouldn't get any attention from you or anyone else. If you end it because your child is calling out for you, they'll learn they can get out of breaktime by repeating this behaviour. While it might seem like hard work, it's best to persevere with breaktime, waiting for your child to be calm and quiet before taking them out. This will pay off in the long term.

> 'My child starts throwing things and screaming when they're in breaktime. Is it okay to check on them?'

If your child discovers they can get a response from you by behaving in a certain way, they'll keep doing it. If you absolutely must check on your child during breaktime, do it quickly with a minimum of fuss. If you find you have to remove dangerous items like scissors or glass, do this without giving your child any attention. It can be hard, but if your child learns you mean what you say, they'll stop behaving like this.

> 'What do I do if my child tries to leave breaktime before the set amount of time?'

It's important to end breaktime when your child has been quiet and calm for the set amount of time. If they keep trying to leave, you have a few options depending on what works best for your family. You can keep returning your child to breaktime as many times as it takes for them to complete a full breaktime. Do this calmly and without fuss, reminding them that breaktime starts when they're in the designated area. You could get a visual timer for your child to know how long breaktime will last.

Another approach could be to warn your child if they don't go to breaktime, they will lose a privilege, such as some of their screen time. Alternatively, you could say, although breaktime is usually 3 minutes, if they go now, the timer will only run for 2 minutes. You know your family best, so go with what works for your child.

'What happens if I lose track of time and leave my kid in breaktime for longer?'

Breaktime is about teaching your child to manage their emotions. As soon as they've done their allotted time, they should come out, so you should stay close to them to monitor when they calm down. Just as a timer can work for your child, you might also like to have one for you so you don't lose track of time.

'I'm worried that breaktime will make my child think I don't care about them.'

When you've been using breaktime consistently, children soon learn it's better to have fun with you than go to breaktime for misbehaviour. In fact, there is research to show when used correctly, it's a highly effective way to improve your child's behaviour and improve your relationship.[29] There is no evidence to show that breaktime used correctly will harm your relationship or make your child more anxious or worried.

To see whether breaktime is working, you should keep track of how often you need to use the strategy for a few weeks. If it's working, you'll see your child in breaktime for brief periods and you'll be using it less and less.

You may find the first time you use breaktime, it takes as long as an hour for your child to be calm for the required amount of time, but this will gradually reduce. Start using breaktime on a day when you know you'll have the time to spare to see it through. Also consider what behaviours you feel breaktime should be used for before you start using it.

direction strategies for older children

When your children hit puberty, their bodies go through some major physical changes. These bring with them a greater need for independence and a heightened emotional sensitivity. This is when they *really* start pushing the boundaries. If you think you had it hard during the terrible twos, I hate to say it, but you haven't seen anything! You may well see increased conflict and tension within the home and may need to adjust your approach.

Many of the strategies you've been using with your younger children can still work with older ones. Descriptive praise, affection, tangible rewards and your time will all support your child, even if you adjust what these are.

Likewise, ignoring minor misbehaviour, counting to 3, stop/start instructions and household rules are also still applicable. However, other strategies like breaktime are no longer appropriate, so I'm going to give you a few alternatives.

Establish clear expectations for behaviour with household rules. Again, keep them small in number, realistic, age-appropriate and applicable to the entire family. Continue to build your relationship with your teen to lower tension and resistance. Think of things you can do together you'll both enjoy. I know of plenty of families whose teens like going on a dog walk with their parent or sitting around with face masks on! You could take up a new hobby together, play sports, go to museums or the movies – there are so many options with your teen child as you start to connect on a more adult level. Make sure you still continue to give your child your undivided attention and show interest in what's going on in their life.

When your teenager misbehaves, the main strategies are still the same – stay calm, consistent and quick while keeping things quiet and boring, although breaktime is no longer an option.

If your child is pushing boundaries or breaking household rules, bring it to their attention and give them the chance to behave differently following these simple steps:

1. **Get their attention.** Keep your voice calm and your focus fixed as you ensure your child pays attention to you.
2. **Give a stop/start instruction** such as, 'Stop shouting and start speaking to me in a calm voice.'
3. **Repeat the instruction** if your teen does not follow it. Keep your tone calm and neutral.
4. **Provide a consequence.** If your teen persists in their behaviour, you'll need to tell them what the consequence will be. It might be they need to remove themselves from the situation until they can speak to you calmly. Keep the consequence appropriate to the situation. Keep it linked to the misbehaviour if you can. For example, if your child breaks something, they need to fix it or do chores to work off the cost of repairs. If they use more credit on their phone than agreed, their credit is reduced the following month. If there isn't an appropriate consequence available, another option is to remove privileges such as take away their phone, television or electronic devices. "Task specific" consequences are when your child has to demonstrate a desired behaviour to earn back their privileges. For example, if a house rule is to do your own laundry and your child is allowed to play their Xbox for 30 minutes, you reduce their Xbox time to 15 minutes until they do their laundry for a week. If at the end of that week they still aren't doing their laundry, you can remove privileges completely until they've consistently done it

for a week. Establish consequences in advance so your teen understands what will happen.
5. **Reconnect.** Once your teen has demonstrated the appropriate behaviour, praise and reward them. The best reward is to spend time doing something you both enjoy – you're showing your teen you enjoy spending time with them when they're just being themselves.
6. **Problem solve.** It might be that you need to talk more about the reasons why your teen misbehaved. Keep discussions in the context of family rules. Have this talk at a later date when you're both feeling calm and can talk about what gave rise to the behaviour and what can be done in future to avoid them recurring.

Problem solving meetings allow your teen to discuss their experiences and work with you to identify solutions. First of all, you should identify the problem and see what needs to change. It's best to work on one problem at a time, so if there seems to be more than one, decide on which is the most important to prioritise.

Next, brainstorm possible solutions together. Be creative – no idea is off the table! Discuss all your suggested solutions and think about how effective it's likely to be, how appropriate it is and whether it will give rise to any other problems. When you're done, choose a solution together.

Once you've decided on a solution, you need to come up with a plan of action so you both know what to do when/if the problem recurs. If it does, review how the solution worked, which gives you another opportunity to show you care about your teen and to strengthen your bond.

Agreement contracts are another way in which you can motivate positive behaviour and are a good way to tackle ongoing misbehaviour. This should be a clear agreement that identifies ideal behaviours, motivators for good behaviour and what the consequences will be for misbehaviour. These work best when drafted with your teen and need regular reviews.

If you have concerns about whether your teen's misbehaviour is outside normal ranges, or it's impacting on the family, you might want to consider professional help. If you suspect there are problems with substance abuse or your child's behaviour is escalating at school, a good first port of call is the school counsellor who may have additional strategies and suggestions for how you can manage the situation.

action steps

- Hold a family meeting specifically for agreeing to the family rules. Start with 5 or 6.
- Regularly review your rules. Update any that no longer apply.
- Arrange a family meeting to role play breaktime with your children. You might like to have the children pretend to be you and you be the child so they can see exactly what's expected and have fun while you're doing it.
- Once you know your child understands how breaktime works, introduce it as a direction strategy.
- Track your progress with breaktime. If you feel it's necessary, hold problem solving meetings with other primary caregivers.
- Adjust your direction strategies as your child gets older. Remember – it's not about discipline so much as redirecting your child's behaviour.
- Don't be afraid to seek professional help if you have any concerns about your child's behaviour.

CHAPTER NINE

the focused family toolbox – trying to keep it together!

> *When all else fails, there's always delusion – Conan O'Brien*

I have a reputation with my clients of being calm, cool and collected in the face of even the most challenging of situations. At some point, they always ask me what my secret is. My reply is that it's pretty simple – I have an ability to remain detached from trauma. That, and my little stash of sedatives.

Over the years, I've had clients tell me about their various coping strategies, some more appropriate than others. Much as I joke about needing a glass of Mummy's Ribena at the end of the day (otherwise known as wine), the reality is that relying on crutches like this isn't healthy. That's not to disparage those who are on prescribed medication to help them deal with their mental health – sometimes this is the absolute best thing you can do for yourself. But if you're finding yourself pouring yourself a glass of wine every night, a glass that gets larger and larger, you really need to be thinking of alternative, less self-destructive ways of keeping it together.

One client, Nora, got so frustrated with her toddler throwing tantrums all the time that one day she threw herself to the floor next to her little girl, Taylor, and screamed right along with her.

'Kicking and punching the floor was really therapeutic!' she told me.

Taylor was so surprised at what her mum was doing that she immediately stopped her tantrum and went to see what was wrong with her mum. As much as Nora was tempted to do this every time Taylor got upset, she knew it wasn't really a good way of dealing with tantrums. However, it gave her an idea that worked really well.

When Taylor was starting to get upset, Nora would sit on the floor with her. This had a double effect – it meant Taylor would be intrigued by what Nora was doing and Nora was forced to stop what she was doing and give all her attention to Taylor. Remember, we're looking at ways to direct your child rather than discipline them and most misbehaviour comes from wanting your attention.

Sitting on the floor meant Nora was on Taylor's level, so she could give her a kiss and cuddle. They could talk about what was upsetting Taylor and tantrums were headed off at the pass. Win-win!

Kids tend to be cranky when they're hungry or tired. When this happens, giving them something to snack on often lifts their mood. It's not just children who get "hangry" either – we adults don't do well on an empty stomach.

A friend of mine, Marie, told me a funny story when her oldest son, Seth, was around 2. She'd bought herself a much-needed chocolate bar. She'd been making some lunch for him, but while he was off playing with his toys, she thought she could have a sneaky snack. She'd just sat down in the kitchen to eat it out of eyesight of her son when he came running in. Inwardly, she sighed. Couldn't she just enjoy her chocolate this one time without anyone bothering her?

But then a brainwave hit her. She told Seth there was a cat in the garden. He loved animals, so ran to the window to see it.

'There's nothing there, Mummy,' he said, disappointed.

'It must have run off,' Marie said, but the little distraction had given her enough time to do what she needed – to grab a carrot stick from the bowl on the table. She put the carrot behind the chocolate bar so it looked like it was sticking out of the packaging.

When her son reached for the chocolate bar, she let him take the carrot. He gave her a look as if to say, *I can't believe she's letting me take her food,* as he gradually pulled out the carrot.

Genuinely believing he'd just stolen his mum's treat, Seth happily toddled off to eat the carrot, leaving Marie to enjoy her chocolate in peace.

Kylie, a client of mine, was getting fed up with never knowing where her 9- and 11-year-olds were. She really missed the days when they'd play games together or go for walks. Now whenever she tried to get them to go out exploring together, the children always said they were too busy to go anywhere.

'What could a tween be doing that makes them too busy to spend time with me?' she complained. 'They've forced me to do the only thing I can think of to get their attention – turn off the internet. It's the one thing guaranteed to make them come running to find me!'

It's not just kids who need breaktime. There are times when I put myself in breaktime just to get a few minutes to centre myself before going back to deal with my darling Grace. With her being so little and me being a single mum, it can be difficult to get away, but that's why I go to my happy place in my mind. I go back to a time before I had Grace when I was able to spend days sunbathing at the beach without a care in the world. In my mind's eye I see the cloudless blue sky, hear the gentle susurration of the waves crashing against the shore, feel the sand between my fingers and toes. Bliss! In fact, excuse me for a moment while I go back there.

The best thing about doing this is that I can still be in the room with Grace so I can keep half an eye on her, but she has no idea that in my mind I'm having a bit of peace and quiet reliving a precious, relaxing memory.

Jenny, a client of mine, has a teen daughter, Autumn, who is really pushing the boundaries right now. Jenny was putting herself in breaktime more and more. Her favourite place to be? Hiding in the pantry, having an essential biscuit or few. She was supposed to be on a diet, but she told me if she didn't treat herself when she needed, she'd be in screaming rows with Autumn all the time.

As we talked, Jenny revealed these sneaky biscuits were increasing in frequency and her diet had all but gone out of the window. It had become a habit, so she was hiding in the pantry even if she wasn't having problems with Autumn.

One day, she'd treated herself to a particularly luscious cake. As soon as she got home, she went straight for the pantry to eat it. The cake was stuffed to overflowing with cream but, since no one was watching, Jenny didn't care that she was getting cream all over her face and fingers – all the more fun licking them clean when she was done.

Jenny was so caught up in the cake, she didn't hear Autumn come home from school. The first thing Autumn did was go to the pantry to get a snack. When she opened the door to find her mum covered in cream, she was horrified.

'Mum! I thought you were meant to be on a diet?'

When I first started putting my program together, I was going to call it the Focused Parenting Formula, but it soon became apparent that if parents were really going to get the results they wanted from any parenting program, it was essential they worked together as a team. It's very confusing for a child when parents practise conflicting parenting strategies or one's always the good cop and the other the bad cop. Everyone needs to be working together for families to flourish, which is why I decided to call my program the Focused **Family** Formula.

Throughout this book, I've been guiding you through a number of team building strategies to build connection with your child. Approaches like holding family meetings, practising undivided attention and empathetic listening and setting household rules, all support you to bond more closely with your child.

In these final couple of chapters, we're going to look more closely at how you can work with your partner or other parent and other primary caregivers, to provide consistency to your child across all your communication, rules, values and routines.

One simple, but important, way for you to stay on the same page with the other parent of your child is to take 10 minutes every day to talk about your children. If you're separated, try to make time to have a phone conversation every week or fortnight to talk about what's happening in your child's life. Schedule these discussions at a time that is convenient for both of you so you can give your undivided attention to each other without feeling like you're rushed or missing out on something. After dinner, or after the kids have gone to bed, tends to work well.

To get the most out of your checking in discussions, they should follow a structure:[30]

1. Ask open-ended questions and look at positive encounters as well as any situations that need work.
2. Practise empathetic listening and don't interrupt the other person or assume you know what they're going to say.
3. Ask what your child's behaviour has been like when you weren't there.
4. If there were no problems, give positive feedback.
5. If there were problems, ask your partner how they dealt

with them. Again, listening without interrupting and without judgement.
6. Give positive feedback on what worked, even if it was heavy going.
7. If need be, schedule a follow up problem-solving meeting.

A problem-solving meeting gives you the chance to identify and talk about specific problem behaviours so you can make a joint decision on the best strategies to use to deal with it.

The structure for a problem-solving meeting is slightly different to a checking in discussion:[31]

1. Arrange a good time for this problem-solving meeting. The most important thing here is that you don't get distracted, so you'll want to be sure you won't be interrupted by the children or anyone else. These discussions need your full concentration and operation.
2. First of all, agree on **one** problem behaviour you're going to focus on. Don't confuse the issue by trying to take on too much at once.
3. Once you've clearly defined the problem, the next step is to come up with a list of all possible solutions. There's never one way to deal with an issue and every child is different, so what works with one child won't necessarily work for another. Work together to brainstorm as many possible solutions as you can come up with. Don't worry about choosing one at this stage – this is all about exploring your options.
4. When you've finished your list of ideas, discuss each solution in turn. Look at how effective it's likely to be, whether it's appropriate for your child and what problems may occur when you start using it with your child. You might like to write down a pros and cons list as you work through your ideas.
5. Working as a team, choose the best solution. Don't be too closely wedded to your preferred solution – you may need

to compromise. Remember you want to do the best thing for your child.
6. Once you've made your decision, put together a plan of action so you both know what to do when the problem behaviour crops up. If your plan doesn't have your expected outcome, don't be discouraged. Have another problem-solving discussion to come up with a different approach.

If you are separated or divorced, communication with your ex-partner is just as important as it always was, if not more so. I know how difficult it can be to navigate this situation. Every relationship is different. You may be lucky enough to have a positive relationship with your ex, but things may not be so great between you. The most important thing to remember is that consistency is crucial for your children, especially now that they are adjusting to parents living separately. If you really can't agree on how you want to raise your children and the subject causes nothing but arguments between you, I strongly suggest you work with a family and relationship counsellor.

It's important you do your best to come to a consensus over how you're going to bring up your children, regardless of circumstance. A united front goes a long way towards successful focused parenting.

dealing with common problems

- **Disagreeing over household rules.** If the pair of you are having difficulties in agreeing on the household rules, don't worry. This is perfectly normal and often a reflection of how you had different upbringings. However, you'll need to find a way to agree because these different expectations send mixed signals to your children, which will then lead to problem behaviours. I recommend sitting down and having an involved discussion over the what, where, how and why of your household rules so you can understand where the other is coming from and both be happy with whatever your agreed plan turns out to be.

- **Disagreeing over discipline.** When you can't agree on the best way to discipline your children, this makes things confusing for them and risks making one of you the good guy and the other one the bad. This, in turn, will lead to your child attempting to play you off against each other. If your family rules are going to have the effect you want, you need to present a united front on a consistent basis.
- **Arguing in front of the children.** Don't worry – I'm not expecting you to be perfect and never argue! Disagreements are a normal part of the human experience. It's how you deal with them that makes all the difference. Arguing in front of your children can have a highly negative effect on them, especially if you argue a lot or you get very heated.[32] If your children see you regularly yelling at each other or ignoring each other, they'll copy you. Children always do what you do, not what you say. If your household rules say, "Use your quiet voice," but you're shouting all the time, it teaches them that not only are you a hypocrite, but also the best way to get what they want is to yell. It undoes all your hard work. Try to use any disagreements as a chance to model good conflict resolution skills. Listen to your partner, keep your cool and be constructive rather than negative.

When your children are misbehaving, you need to stay calm to follow your agreed distraction strategy. If your partner is dealing with the situation, resist the urge to interfere. Only get involved if they ask for your help. Back each other up and stay with your agreed approach – this is why having those regular meetings is so important. When you know in advance how you're going to tackle any given situation, it becomes much easier to put that plan into practice.

When the incident has been resolved, find a moment to talk about what happened, giving each other constructive feedback. If the situation requires a more in-depth analysis, schedule a problem-solving meeting.

being the calm in the chaos

For all my serene demeanour, I know all too well that one of the biggest challenges for parents is staying calm in the face of provocation. Trust me – you're not alone in wanting to forget about being a good parent and scream along with your child. I've had more than my fair share of moments of wanting to throw away all the parenting books and tell the meditation gurus just where they can stick their breathing exercises. So it's not just you!

But the reality is those breathing exercises have been proven by science to help regulate your emotions and decrease the symptoms of stress.[33] When you feel anxious, your breathing becomes rapid and shallow, which can increase your heart rate, make you feel dizzy and lightheaded or nauseous and you may sweat.

Keeping your breathing under control when you're under stress reduces the fight or flight responses. Here's 3 ways you can calm your breath – and yourself – down when you're feeling anxious:

breathe slowly

Under normal circumstances, when you inhale, your heart rate speeds up slightly and then slows as you exhale. When you consciously breathe in and out for longer than usual, you feel less stressed and more relaxed because your heart rate slows.

This is a short exercise known as box breathing that you can do at any time. I recommend doing it multiple times a day.

The more you do it, the more you'll feel comfortable using it in difficult situations to calm and quieten your mind.

- Inhale slowly and deeply through your nose for a count of 4 seconds. Fill your lungs as much as possible, letting your stomach rise with the breath.
- Once you've counted to 4 and your lungs are full, hold your breath for a count of 4.
- Exhale gently and slowly through your mouth for a count of 4. As you breathe out, let go of any tension you may be holding in your body.
- Hold your breath for a count of 4 then start all over again.

Doing this quick and simple exercise for just a few rounds will slow your breathing and help you stay calm.

count backwards

We've all heard the advice of counting to 10 before you lose your temper. This is because when you do something to distract your mind from the present moment, focusing on it completely for just a few seconds, your stress levels lower.

I prefer to count backwards, and I use this technique regularly, especially when Grace has decided to use my lipstick to draw on the walls or stuff paper down the toilet.

When you first start working with this technique, I recommend going somewhere quiet, closing your eyes and counting backwards for as long as you need. 10 to 1 is fine, but you can start at 20, 30, 40, or whatever you'll need to get your emotions under control. If you feel you need a bigger distraction, try making it a little harder for yourself, such as counting backwards from 100 in 3s.

Once you've found an approach that works for you in a quiet place, you can use it at any time to keep your cool.

be mindfully present

Mindfulness is an increasingly popular way of coping with stress. When you are focused on what is happening in the present moment without judgement, it helps to calm your mind and stop worrying or fretting.

One simple way of doing this is to check in with each of your senses:

- Name 5 things you can see right now.
- Name 4 things you can hear.
- Name 3 things you can feel.
- Name 2 things you can smell. If you can't smell anything, actively go looking for something, such as perfume or flowers. This alone will distract you from the current source of your stress.
- Name 1 thing you can taste. If there's nothing, you could get yourself a drink and focus on that flavour and the feel of the liquid in your mouth.

Paying attention to anything else will anchor you in the present moment, taking your thoughts away from whatever's bothering you.

hold a 3 rs meeting

3 Rs meetings are good for children who are old enough to be able to identify their emotions and describe their behaviour while appreciating the effect these may have on themselves and others. When your child reaches this stage, it can be easy to assume they can now always self-soothe and regulate their emotions, but they've still got a lot of emotional maturing to come. As such, when you try to resolve a situation in the heat of the moment, it all goes horribly wrong, making things worse, not better.

Let's look at a common misuse of breaktime. Let's say your child has just finished breaktime. Instead of doing something neutral together, you start explaining to them what happened in minute detail, going into why you had to count to 3, what they were doing wrong, what they should have done instead and blah, blah, blah. All you're doing is prolonging the agony, undoing all your hard work with breaktime. Just accept their apology, if there even is one, and redirect their attention or go get a glass of water or some other neutral activity.

Rather than discussing what's happened at the time, simply say you'd like to hold a brief 3 Rs meeting later that day. By brief, I really do mean brief – no longer than 5 minutes. Set them for a time when you know your child will be calm and relaxed. A good idea is to set a timer for these meetings, especially with younger children, and have something fun planned for afterwards. That way you don't get caught up in long, drawn-out conversations and you've already got a way to redirect their attention once the meeting's done.

A 3 Rs meeting has 3 simple steps. It gives your child the chance to explain their version of what happened, how they felt and what they would like to do differently next time. Continue to practise empathetic listening, using open ended questions without judgement.

- **Reflect:** What happened? How did you react?
- **Realise:** How did this make you feel?
- **Resolve:** What do you think the solution could be? What would you do differently in future?

These 3 Rs meetings give your child the opportunity to take responsibility for their actions without putting any pressure on them and helps them to learn more effective ways of dealing with difficult situations in the future.

action steps

- If you're struggling to keep your cool, feel free to go to my website www.deborahbyrne.com and listen to, or download, my specially designed stress relief track.
- You can also get other tools for dealing with stress as well as more information about the Focus Family Formula on my website.
- Start using checking-in and problem-solving meetings if your child is old enough.
- Try out the 3 calming exercises outlined in this chapter to see which ones are best for you. Once you've decided on your preference(s), start practising them on a regular basis. Remember to do them when you're not feeling stressed as well as during tough situations for maximum benefit.
- When your child is old enough to reflect on their emotions, start having 3 Rs meetings with them.

CHAPTER TEN

the focused family transition –
one step forward, two steps back

I welcome change as long as nothing is altered or different than before – Unknown

My friend Tara once told me she couldn't catch a break! When her children were little, they'd follow her around all the time so she couldn't even go to the toilet without her little "helpers". When they'd grown out of this phase, they decided to get a puppy. Tara told me that just when her children had stopped insisting on being there when she was in the bathroom, now the puppy follows her there instead!

At least the puppy loved going for long walks. Tara's youngest daughter, Faye, was only happy going out on her own terms. Before she learned to stand properly, Faye wanted to run everywhere, so Tara was constantly having to kiss her bumps and bruises better. But when she got to around 18 months, she wanted to be carried everywhere. It would have been understandable if she was tired, but Faye would walk for

5 minutes and decide she'd rather be travelling first class – in Mummy's arms.

If Tara didn't pick her up, Faye would just plop right down and sit wherever they were, no matter how inconvenient. She wouldn't check to see what she was sitting in either, so Tara had to do a fair few extra washes when Faye sat in something particularly nasty. Faye didn't care. As long as she got what she wanted, nothing else mattered.

Nicole, a client of mine, had two children – Kacey, aged 10 and Kevin, aged 9. One day, she went to the garage where they kept their deep freezer to get some food for dinner. The children thought it would be funny to lock their mum in. To this day, she has no idea which one turned the key, but both of them thought it was hilarious listening to their mum banging on the door, freaking out about what mischief they might be getting up to while they had free reign of the house.

Eventually, Nicole managed to find a screwdriver and unlock the door. It had maybe taken her 15-20 minutes to escape the garage, but it felt like forever to the panicked mum. She found her children in the lounge watching television, having helped themselves to her secret stash of chocolate. Needless to say, she wasn't happy.

Kerry's daughter, Abby, was 10 when her baby brother was born. She hadn't enjoyed making the adjustment from being an only child to big sister and Kerry had come to me to help with Abby's behaviour.

The final straw had been when Kerry had taken Abby to school. She'd been up all night with the baby, so had been rushing to get her daughter out of the door. Still in her pyjamas, she'd left it too late for them to walk to school, so she drove for once and had the baby in the back of the car. They pulled into the dropping off lane outside the school, then Kerry went to give Abby a quick kiss goodbye. Abby folded her arms and looked away.

'Okay,' said Kerry, trying not to lose her temper. 'I guess you're getting a bit too old for kisses. Have a good day at school.'

Abby said nothing, still staring steadfastly out the window.

'Abby, you need to get out of the car and go to school or you're going to be late.'

Abby still wasn't moving, so Kerry got out of the car to go round and open the door. The second she was gone, Abby swiftly moved to lock the car doors, leaving Kerry stuck outside without her keys.

Kerry banged on the window, but Abby simply turned her head away. The baby started crying, making Kerry even more stressed out. Eventually, Kerry had to call her husband to bring the spare car keys. As Abby saw her dad driving towards her, she quickly unlocked the door, got out of the car and raced into school, yelling, 'Goodbye!' over her shoulder.

It really isn't any better for my clients with older children either. A story I hear a lot is that whenever they ask them to do something simple, like put their dirty clothes in the laundry basket, the response is eye rolls, huffs and sighs, slouched body language, all wrapped up with a cry of, 'Don't you think I know I need to pick up my laundry? Jeez, Mum. You don't need to yell at me!'

If yelling means speaking in a reasonable tone of voice, then consider me yelling all the time!

There are moments when the only consolation is it won't be long before they're off to university and then they'll be the ones dealing with sleepless nights, cleaning up vomit and dealing with surly teens.

It's at this point in the book I think it's only fair to warn you that if you think following all the advice I've given you means parenting will be plain sailing, you're in for a shock. Regression is very common in children for various reasons and is a normal part of healthy development. Heck, even adults can regress at times in the right circumstances. So don't think you've got it all figured out if your child's sitting calmly in breaktime, they happily do their chores and they tuck themselves up at bedtime. Tomorrow could be the complete opposite – and it's totally normal.

However, if you've noticed your child regressing, it's always worth considering what may be the cause. It may be a sign of stress in your child due to overwhelm and an inability to deal with their emotions.

When your child goes through a regressive stage, try to keep your attention on the underlying cause of it rather than the actual behaviour. If your child is feeling stressed, they may not have the emotional maturity to deal with it yet so can't display age-appropriate behaviours. It can also be a way of gaining attention, for example, acting like a toddler after the arrival of a baby sibling so they can get more hugs and have any misbehaviour be ignored. These two main causes both need to be tackled appropriately to avoid any further regression.

Another issue may be resistance, which is when your child is misbehaving and challenging any attempt from you to redirect or guide them. They may not want to comply with your redirection strategies or changes to the household routine. This is distinct to regression but still requires you to stay calm and collected as you support your child through the situation. Try to understand the root cause, which will help you deal with the problem and come up with an appropriate solution.

It's perfectly natural to want to see fast results for all your hard work, but when you have unrealistic expectations, you're only setting yourself up for disappointment. This is a long-term process that requires dedication and commitment, the willingness to persevere through the speed bumps in the short term for the sake of long-term gain. The reality is, if you really want to see an improvement in your family dynamics, you have to accept that it will take time. How much time will depend on the age of your children and how ingrained old patterns of behaviour are. As they say, it's not about whether you get knocked down but how often you pick yourself back up.

If you only take one thing away from this book, let it be the important role **consistency** plays. I know families who tried new routines for a few short weeks and gave up when they didn't get permanent, positive change. Going back to their old way of being wasn't going to solve their problems, but it seemed easier than persisting when the going got tough.

I would be doing you a disservice if I didn't warn you that you're going to have good days and bad days, seeing gradual improvements but combined with challenges along the way. It's a little like trying to climb up a sand dune. You can see the summit in sight, you know you're going to get there, but as you make your way up, you're constantly sliding back, so your progress is much slower than you'd like – but there's still progress.

It takes self-discipline to be consistent, but if you can't be consistent, you won't develop the healthy habits required to implement this new style of parenting. You have to be committed to this program if you want to see permanent improvement.

If you follow the advice in this book, you'll have a consistent routine and a set of family rules that work for your family, all of which will reduce stress and the pressure you put yourself under. Think about how things are for you right now. Do you want it to continue? Because that's what will happen if you keep doing things the same way.

Making a change *and being consistent in that change* enables you to focus on outcomes rather than worrying about specific incidents.

Let's say you want to spend more time with your son. When you commit to that goal and are consistent about spending half an hour with him every day, even if it means getting up early for work or not spending so long watching Netflix, you'll soon have a better relationship without you even feeling like it's been a chore. You'll naturally build on this new habit to plan other fun things to do together, and your child will want to spend time with you as much as you want to spend time with them.

The best part of all this is that once you see the difference being consistent makes to your family, you'll be motivated to take that same dedication and apply it to other areas of your life that you feel need to change.

Think about how many things you do every day, almost without thinking about it – brushing your teeth, brushing your hair, getting dressed, scrolling on social media, locking the door behind you when you go out, etc. These are habits that have become ingrained through what? Say it with me – **consistency!** Consider all the changes you're making to your parenting style as part of your new normal. Consistently following your family rules will help you establish good habits until your new approach feels effortless, even though you're working on it every day.

If this all feels a little overwhelming, start small. You don't have to make big changes – in fact, that's more likely to set yourself up for failures. Think about little changes you can make right now that will help you change the direction of your parenting room.

For example, instead of yelling at your child to get out of bed, why don't you take an extra couple of minutes to go to their room and use a calm voice to ask them to get up and have breakfast with you. This starts the day on a much more positive tone and establishes the mood for the day. Just that one little change can then be built upon more and more until you're doing things completely differently to how you are now, but it doesn't feel like it's been an uphill slog to get there.

We've talked before about rewarding your children for their good behaviour with time, attention, praise, etc. but don't forget yourself. You deserve a treat too for all the hard work you're doing! At the end of every week, give yourself a little reward for consistently practising good habits and think about the positive changes you've observed in your family dynamics.

The more self-aware you are around what you are doing and what you would like to do, gradually swapping old habits for new ones, the easier it becomes to integrate them into your family routine. These changes will become automatic in time, becoming effortless rather than hard, taking you closer and closer to becoming the parent you always said you would be.

Finally, I'd like to introduce you to ACT (Acceptance and Commitment Therapy). The fundamental principles of ACT are mindfulness, self-reflection, acceptance and forgiveness. It is a powerful, progressive form of therapy that demonstrates the benefits of self-awareness, enables you to recognise your self-sabotaging ego states and supports you to change your internal dialogue.

Speaking from a personal perspective, adding ACT to my emotional tool kit was a key part of my recovery from parental burnout. Not only did it transform the way I viewed myself, it forced me to live more consciously. When you accept your past, you can enjoy the present moment and look forward to the future.

If you'd like to learn more about ACT, look up the interview between Russ Harris and Dennis Tirch about the Art and Science of Self-Compassion.[34]

action steps

- Maintain an open mind towards your child's behaviour and consider whether they are displaying any signs of resistance or regression. If you notice any, consider what may be the root cause so you can come up with an effective strategy.
- Examine your own parenting approach and identify 3 habits you would like to change. Be consistently dedicated to establishing a new way of doing things. Once you feel you've developed a new habit, expand your list to gradually shift how you're doing things.

CHAPTER ELEVEN

final thoughts

If a child is to keep alive his inborn sense of wonder, he needs the companionship of at least one adult who can share it, rediscovering with him the joy, excitement, and mystery of the world we live in
– Rachel Carson

Confident parents raise confident kids and having read this book, if you put just some of what you've learned into practice, you'll be more confident interacting with your children.

Parenting is hard work. There are days when we just want to run away and hide or curl up under the duvet with a big tub of cookie dough and pretend the children aren't out there needing us. But now you have the tools you need to cope with those days.

Having gone through this book you may have concerns that your child is displaying signs of feeling anxious or depressed, having problems that are outside normal behaviour. How do you know when your child needs support and at what point do you look for professional help?

These are some situations when I'd always advise parents to get appropriate support:
- Your child is facing a major life change, such as parents separating, starting a new school, moving house, or gaining a sibling.
- Your child's behaviour seems to be getting worse as they get older instead of improving.
- Your child is physically violent and can't seem to self-regulate for long, if at all.
- Your child has experienced a traumatic event, such as the death of a loved one, being involved in a serious accident (or someone they're close to being involved in one), abuse or anything else that has negatively impacted on their emotional wellbeing.
- Your child's personality changes drastically without explanation. They may become withdrawn, less social, stop going out with their friends or start skipping school.
- Your child's anxiety seems greater than other children their age and it impacts on their ability to concentrate or complete everyday activities such as going to school, doing their homework, sitting down to meals or settling down at night.
- Your child is struggling in school with poor grades, finding it hard to concentrate or struggling to make friends or behave appropriately.

If you recognise your child in the above list, or you have any other concerns, please be aware there is absolutely **no** shame or embarrassment in getting help for your child's mental health and wellbeing. You'd take them to the doctor if they broke a bone, right? It's just as important to get help if your child's mental health is suffering or there's another undiagnosed cause, such as ADHD.

Just like you, your children will experience difficult times, as much as we want to wrap them up in cotton wool and protect them from all the bad things in the world. They deserve to feel supported and have someone to talk to and that person might not always be you. That's okay. You're doing a great job in getting them the help they need.

The one thing I've learned as a parent is there are two of you in the equation and no matter how much you think you've got things sorted, your child will always find a way of throwing you a curve ball. Give yourself permission to feel vulnerable at times and practise kindness to yourself. Forgive yourself your mistakes – you're only human. Nobody expects you to be perfect, not even your children. Welcome any challenges as learning opportunities sent to take you further down the path to self-discovery.

Parenting is a wild and bumpy ride. Your children will teach you things you never knew. It's an incredibly rewarding role that will teach you so much about the person you are and the person you can be. Strap in and enjoy the journey for what it is – blink and it'll all be over.

Pat yourself on the back and tell yourself that you're an incredible parent, because you really are. **You are amazing!**

action steps

- Don't be afraid to seek professional help if you're feeling overwhelmed or you feel your child needs more support and expertise than you're in a position to provide.
- Come back to this book as often as you need to for reminders and strategies. Just reading this in the first place is a sign of what a great parent you are. Keep up that dedication as you start implementing everything you've learned and building on your progress.
- Be consistent! It's the one thing your children really need from you to support them into growing into the awesome human beings they were born to be.

- Keep putting one foot in front of the other and you'll get to where you want to go. We tend to overestimate what we can achieve in a week and underestimate what we can do in a year. As long as you're making progress every day, no matter how small, you'll see the results of your hard work sooner or later.

GLOSSARY

ACT (Acceptance and Commitment Therapy) – a progressive form of therapy that focuses on self-awareness, allowing you to identify your self-sabotaging ego states and change your internal dialogue.

Breaktime – an alternative to timeout that removes attention from your child to redirect their behaviour.

Checking in discussions – a regular conversation about your children to track progress and ensure you and other caregivers are on the same page.

DISC scale – Four main personality types that shape how you communicate:

    Panther or dominance – action oriented, leader types.

    Peacock or influence – outgoing optimists who love being around people.

    Dolphin or steadiness – people pleasers who want to have fun.

    Owl or conscientiousness – natural diplomats who are driven by logic.

Empathetic listening – the act of consciously listening without judgement.

Escalation trap – A situation where both child and parent escalate their behaviour, resulting in highly strung emotions and negative behaviour.

Family meeting – a regular meeting where everyone discusses their problems and plans the week ahead.

The 4 Ds Funnel System – a way of prioritising your to-do list.

Non-violent communication (NVC) – developed by Marshall B. Rosenburg, NVC involves communicating honestly and receiving with empathy.

Problem solving meeting – a follow up to checking in discussions where you collectively identify solutions to problems and agree a strategy moving forward.

Reticular Activating System (RAS) – the part of the brain that validates your beliefs.

3 Rs Meeting – a brief meeting held a while after a challenging situation that gives your child a chance to reflect on what happened and what they can do differently in the future.

SUGGESTED READING

- *Do Less* by Kate Northrup, published by Hay House Inc
- *Simplicity Parenting* by Kim John Payne, published by Ballantine
- *The Book You Wish Your Parents Had Read* by Philippa Perry, published by Penguin
- *123 Magic* by Thomas W. Phelan, published by Parent Magic Inc
- *Confident Parents, Confident Kids* by Jennifer S. Miller, published by Fair Winds Press
- *The Whole Brain Child* by Daniel J. Siegel, published by Bantam
- *The Conscious Parent* by Shefali Tsabary, published by Namaste Publishing
- *Nonviolent communication* by Marshall Rosenburg, published by PuddleDancer Press

ENDNOTES

introduction

1 https://www.healthline.com/nutrition/12-benefits-of-meditation

chapter one

2 https://www.apa.org/topics/mindfulness/meditation
3 https://www.ncbi.nlm.nih.gov/pmc/articles/PMC3303565/
4 https://academic.oup.com/sleep/article/37/9/1553/2416992
5 https://www.youtube.com/c/davidjimeditation
6 https://e360.yale.edu/features/ecopsychology-how-immersion-in-nature-benefits-your-health
7 https://www.sciencealert.com/just-looking-at-photos-of-nature-could-be-enough-to-lower-your-work-stress-levels

chapter two

8 https://www.forbes.com/sites/emmajohnson/2015/04/20/study-proves-moms-spend-too-much-time-with-their-kids-liberates-working-moms-everywhere/?sh=20f843334edc
9 https://www.ted.com/talks/laura_vanderkam_how_to_gain_control_of_your_free_time?language=en
10 https://www.cdc.gov/media/releases/2016/p0215-enough-sleep.html#:~:text=More%20than%20a%20third%20of,Morbidity%20and%20Mortality%20Weekly%20Report.

chapter three

11 https://en.wikipedia.org/wiki/DISC_assessment

chapter four

12 https://www.verywellmind.com/the-best-stress-relief-3144573

chapter five

13 https://www.additudemag.com/is-adhd-hereditary-blog/
14 https://www.cornerstonesforparents.com/4-goals-misbehavior
15 https://ijccep.springeropen.com/articles/10.1186/s40723-017-0038-6
16 https://www.whattoexpect.com/first-year/week-10/decoding-cries.aspx
17 https://www.curiousneuron.com/childdevelopmentarticles/2016/8/23/why-we-should-all-learn-to-refrain-from-arguing-in-front-of-a-baby
18 https://drdansiegel.com/

chapter six

19 https://www.ncbi.nlm.nih.gov/pmc/articles/PMC6306969/
20 https://docs.wixstatic.com/ugd/c8fe6e_65448e5da9754a6c8676f179d07067d1.pdf
21 https://blog.valleywisehealth.org/negative-effect-of-screen-time-adults-children/

chapter seven

22 https://www.123magic.com/about-us.html
23 https://www.sciencedaily.com/releases/2016/01/160118134938.htm
24 https://www.amazon.com/Nonviolent-Communication-Language-Life-Guides/dp/189200528X
25 https://www.nonviolentcommunication.com/pdf_files/4part_nvc_process.pdf

chapter eight

26 https://www.canr.msu.edu/news/are_there_problems_with_just_saying_no_to_kids
27 https://childmind.org/article/are-time-outs-harmful-kids/
28 https://www.livescience.com/55932-how-to-make-timeouts-work-for-your-kids.html
29 https://www.washingtonpost.com/lifestyle/2018/11/30/when-used-correctly-timeouts-are-an-effective-tool-parents-young-kids/

chapter nine

30 Downloadable PDF chart for checking in discussions: https://bit.ly/2ZXsu60
31 Downloadable PDF chart for problem-solving discussions: https://bit.ly/3bKkSGY
32 https://www.bbc.co.uk/news/education-43486641
33 https://www.frontiersin.org/articles/10.3389/fpsyg.2017.00220/full
34 https://youtu.be/7l6FGG3Aa0g

www.ingramcontent.com/pod-product-compliance
Lightning Source LLC
Chambersburg PA
CBHW012208090526
44583CB00023BA/2983